HIDDEN HISTORY *of* BLACK CINCINNATI

Kareem A. Simpson

THE History PRESS

Published by The History Press
An imprint of Arcadia Publishing
Charleston, SC
www.historypress.com

First published 2026

Manufactured in the United States

ISBN 9781467158138
Hardcover ISBN 9781540299710

Library of Congress Control Number applied for.

Notice: The information in this book is true and complete to the best of our knowledge. It is offered without guarantee on the part of the author or The History Press. The author and The History Press disclaim all liability in connection with the use of this book.

Contents

Preface

Throughout my life, I've roamed the storied streets and hidden corners of Cincinnati, Ohio, chasing the whispers of its history. My mission? To uncover the personal stories that have shaped the city's iconic spaces. As a native son—or close enough, hailing from Northern Kentucky, which is forever intertwined with the greater Cincinnati tapestry—I've spent countless hours exploring this region. From its bustling downtown to its quiet neighborhoods, I've been captivated by the places where past and present meet. These spaces teem with history, but often, they echo with the absence of the stories that resonate most deeply with me.

Take Union Terminal, for instance. One of the last grand train stations built in America, it now houses the Cincinnati Museum Center. For me, though, it's more than just an architectural marvel; it's the real-life inspiration for the Hall of Justice from the *Super Friends* cartoons. Then there's the William Howard Taft National Historic Site, birthplace of our twenty-seventh president and tenth chief justice. Each place is steeped in a narrative that's been polished and presented as a piece of America's collective memory.

Yet as I wandered through these hallowed spaces, an unsettling pattern emerged: the glaring absence of Black stories. Again and again, I found that the tales of triumph, struggle, and resilience from people who looked like me had been erased, sidelined, or relegated to the margins. So, this book was born, a deliberate act to flip the script. It's an exploration of Cincinnati's historic places, told with Black and brown faces at the center of the narrative. It's history, reimagined.

As a self-confessed history nerd—a title I've embraced despite the "coolness" factor it forfeits—I've spent countless hours grappling with questions that refuse to let me rest:

> Was Covington's Eastside really the only major Black community in Northern Kentucky before school desegregation? If so, why?
>
> What were the circumstances surrounding Margaret Garner's escape from slavery to Cincinnati in the mid-1800s? And how was she captured so quickly? Was her freedom truly so fleeting?
>
> We know Boss Cox dominated Cincinnati politics in the early twentieth century, but who were the Black workers and artisans who helped maintain his estate in Clifton? And why don't we know their names?

These questions are my compass, guiding me through the archives and across the city's streets in search of answers.

My love for history began when I was a child in the back seat of my mother's car, her in the driver's seat, ushering me around town. She had a knack for storytelling, weaving tales of Cincinnati and Northern Kentucky as we drove past landmarks and through neighborhoods. But unlike the history books I encountered in school, my mother's stories included the lives of Black Americans, the people who lived, worked, and thrived in spaces history often forgot. She spoke of Black women in hoop skirts bustling through the streets, men forging a living against all odds, children chasing dreams that seemed out of reach. These stories planted a seed in me, one that has grown into a desire to unearth and amplify these forgotten narratives.

There's a peculiar sanitization that occurs when American history is told, a kind of white glove treatment that scrubs away the uncomfortable truths. Cincinnati's history is no different. It's polished to a shine, celebrating the achievements of a select few while relegating entire communities to the shadows. Statues, plaques, and manicured parks commemorate familiar names, but if you peer closer, you'll notice the absence of the Black innovators, dreamers, and builders who made this city great. It's as though history itself has conspired to render them invisible. But this book is here to adjust the lens, to sharpen the focus, and to bring these hidden stories into the light.

Page 12 Wednesday, July 13, 1994 The Recorder Nev

In

Area student learn journalism

Kareem Simpson of Covington, left, and Jocelyn McCoy of Edgewood, third from left, learned the basics of reporting, writing and newspaper design at the High School Minority Workshop at the University of Kentucky June 8-17. They were among 17 students across the state who attended the weeklong session. Both will be seniors at Holmes High School in the fall.

News clipping from the *Lexington Record* of Kareem A. Simpson at summer writing camp for high school students at the University of Kentucky (Lexington, Kentucky), circa 1994. *K.A. Simpson Collection.*

This isn't just a history book, mind you. It's a three-dimensional narrative, a tapestry woven with the threads of personal stories, systemic challenges, and the enduring spirit of a community. We'll delve into how race has been used to consolidate power and perpetuate inequality, and we'll also highlight the ways people have resisted and reimagined these dynamics. It's a journey through time, but it's also a call to action, urging us to understand the past to create a more equitable future.

For me, writing has always been an act of rebellion. It's my way of responding to the gaps and silences I encountered in books, movies, and classrooms. Growing up as a Black child of the 1980s, I rarely saw characters who looked or acted like me at the center of the narrative. Writing became my way of filling that void, of asserting my place in the story. It's been a journey of discovery, not just of the craft but also of myself. Every sentence I write feels like a step forward, a way of claiming space in a world that often tries to box me out.

Audacity is the fuel that keeps me going—the audacity to believe that my words matter, that my perspective is worth sharing, that my stories deserve to be told. This audacity was a gift from my mother, nurtured by the strength and resilience of the Black community that surrounded me. It's an inheritance I carry with pride, and it's what propelled me to write this book.

Politically, our world is at a crossroads today. The Black Lives Matter movement has reignited conversations about systemic racism, and the COVID-19 pandemic has exposed the deep inequities that continue to plague our society. These challenges demand that we confront uncomfortable truths, that we examine the systems and structures that have perpetuated injustice for far too long. This book is my contribution to that conversation, a reminder that the benefits we enjoy today were built on the backs of communities who were too often ignored and undervalued.

But let's not stop there. This book is also a celebration, a recognition of the extraordinary resilience, creativity, and innovation that Black Cincinnatians have brought to this region. It's about the musicians who filled the air with

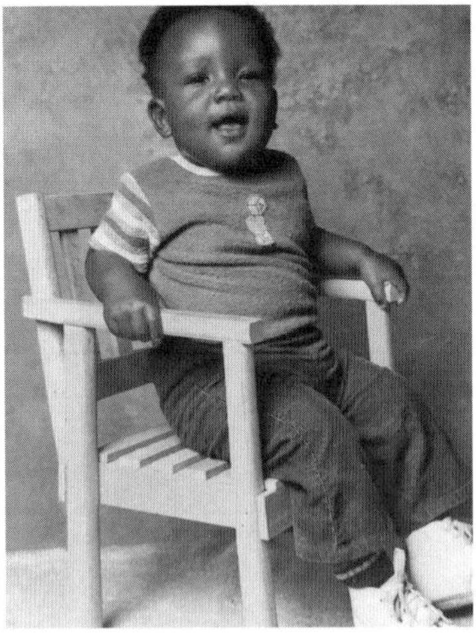

Kareem A. Simpson at the age of one. *K.A. Simpson Collection.*

jazz and the blues, the entrepreneurs who built businesses from the ground up, and the activists who marched for justice, demanding a seat at the table. It's about the mothers and fathers who worked tirelessly to provide for their families, the educators who inspired generations of students, and the artists who used their talents to reflect the beauty and struggle of the Black experience.

As we journey through the historic spaces and places of Cincinnati and Northern Kentucky, I invite you to see them through a new lens. Imagine the stories that these spaces hold, the laughter, the tears, the dreams, and the struggles. Picture the people who walked these streets, who left their mark on this city, even if history has tried to erase them. Let's honor their legacy and ensure that their stories are never forgotten again.

So, buckle up, because we're about to embark on a journey that's equal parts history lesson and love letter. It's a journey that challenges us to see the past for what it truly was, to acknowledge the sacrifices and contributions of those who came before us, and to carry their stories forward into the future. Together, we'll uncover the hidden history of Cincinnati and Northern Kentucky, and in doing so, we'll shine a light on the incredible people who made this region what it is today.

ACKNOWLEDGEMENTS

Writing *Hidden History of Black Cincinnati* has been a journey of discovery, reflection, and profound appreciation for the rich history that surrounds us. I am deeply grateful to the Kenton County Library, Cincinnati Museum Center and the Taft Museum of Art for their generosity in providing the photographs that bring this book to life. Their collections are invaluable resources that help preserve the spirit of our community.

Most importantly, I extend my heartfelt gratitude to my mother, Dr. Katherine D. Simpson. It was she who instilled in me a love of history and the art of storytelling, fostering my curiosity and encouraging me to explore the stories that shape who we are. Her influence is woven into every page of this work, and I am endlessly thankful for her guidance, wisdom, and the example she set.

Thank you to everyone who helped make this project a reality and to all the readers who embark on this journey with me.

1

Northern Kentucky's Devou Park and Cincinnati's West End Neighborhood

There's a certain charm to Cincinnati that baffles and beguiles newcomers. It's a city that doesn't give up all its secrets at once, but when it does, oh, how rich the rewards are. Did you know that Cincinnati once wore the nickname "Porkopolis" with pride? Or that flying into Cincinnati means you're actually landing in Northern Kentucky? Yes, the Cincinnati/Northern Kentucky International Airport sits just south of the Ohio River, a delightful bit of irony that underscores how deeply interconnected the two regions truly are.

In the early nineteenth century, this area was a booming epicenter of commerce and opportunity. The Ohio River, a vast and winding artery, connected Cincinnati and Northern Kentucky to the broader world. For American settlers heading west, the river was a lifeline. It brought goods, people, and dreams to this bustling hub, where steamboats paused for repairs and travelers refreshed themselves at the many taverns, inns, and eateries that sprang up along its banks. The region's economic vitality was amplified by the Miami Erie Canal, which flowed southward from northwestern Ohio to Cincinnati, creating a crucial route for farmers to transport their goods to market with remarkable efficiency.

It was in this fertile ground of commerce and ingenuity that Cincinnati's claim to "Porkopolis" emerged. Farmers flocked to the city to sell their livestock, where it was slaughtered, processed, and shipped to settlers moving westward or to markets across the burgeoning United States. Cincinnati became the meatpacking capital of the country, its name now synonymous

William P. Devou House, Behringer Crawford Museum, circa 1910–24. *Kenton County Public Library*.

with the pig industry. It wasn't just about economic might, though; this era also heralded Cincinnati as a burgeoning cultural and intellectual hub.

Daniel Drake, a visionary physician, founded the Medical College of Ohio in 1819 to elevate medical care on what was then considered the frontier. Cincinnati also served as a literary and ideological flashpoint. Harriet Beecher Stowe, who called the city home, used her experiences here to inform her groundbreaking work, *Uncle Tom's Cabin*, a novel that exposed the horrors of slavery to a global audience. It was no coincidence that abolitionists from around the nation converged on Cincinnati. Situated across the Ohio River from Kentucky, a slaveholding state, the city became a beacon of hope and resistance. Antislavery newspapers and tracts published in Cincinnati found their way into the hands of readers across the country, fueling the fight for freedom.

To understand Cincinnati, you must also consider its quieter counterpart, Covington, Kentucky. Located just across the river, Covington offers one of the most breathtaking views of downtown Cincinnati. From the hilltop of Devou Park, the city's skyline rises like a promise, reflecting the resilience

William P. Devou Jr., circa 1912. *From the* Cincinnati Post.

and complexity of the region. Devou Park, with its lush greenery and sweeping panoramas, is one of the jewels of Northern Kentucky. It offers trails, golf courses, and cultural landmarks like the Behringer-Crawford Museum, yet its story is entwined with the lives of the Black Americans who labored and lived on its land long before it became a public space.

Devou Park's origins date back to 1910, when William P. and Charles P. Devou donated five hundred acres to the City of Covington. But the story of this land stretches farther into the past. Before the Devou family's ownership, it was a patchwork of parcels, many held by slave-owning families who relied on the labor of Black men and women to build their wealth. Some landowners even mentioned their enslaved laborers in their wills, leaving behind a paper trail that offers a glimpse into the lives of the people whose contributions remain largely unrecognized.

One such landowner was Reverend William Montague, who acquired seven hundred acres in 1833. Montague was not just a man of faith; he was also a man of influence. As the pastor of Covington's Fifth Street Christian Church and a teacher at a local academy for boys, Montague held a prominent position in the community. His familial ties only added to his stature; his distant relative Richard Mentor Johnson served as vice president of the United States under Martin Van Buren. Incidentally, Richard Mentor Johnson carried on a long, very public common-law marriage with Julia Chinn—a Black woman who, despite being his partner in every sense of the word, remained legally enslaved throughout their life together. It's a fascinating and complicated love story, but that tale, dear reader, I'll tuck away for the next book.

In November 1839, Montague expanded his holdings with an additional 220 acres, part of what is now Devou Park. Among the people listed in Montague's household were John, a twenty-three-year-old Black laborer, and Carolyn, an eighteen-year-old Black domestic servant. Their presence on this land marks the first documented connection between Black Americans and what would later become Devou Park.

When Montague passed away on July 12, 1842, he left behind a will that revealed a complicated legacy. Written just a day before his death, the

Aerial photo of Cincinnati's West End neighborhood. *Kenton County Public Library.*

document ordered the freedom of one enslaved individual, Armsted, and the continued care of another, Mariah. The act of freeing Armsted—a monumental decision at the time—raises questions about Montague's beliefs and the societal pressures he faced. Was this an act of conscience, or was it born of a deeper, unspoken bond?

The following is a portion of Montague's will:

> *I also will and direct that my black man Armsted be liberated and set free at the close of the year eighteen hundred and fifty provided my wife*

> *is not living at that time, otherwise to remain in servitude or service until her death. And as the old Black woman Mariah has enjoyed her liberty or freedom for many years I wish her to do the same during her life and that my children mutually and equally see to her so as not to let her suffer for want of attention.*

The stories of people like John, Carolyn, Armsted, and Mariah are fragments of a larger mosaic. They remind us that the land we now enjoy for leisure and recreation was once a site of labor, struggle, and resilience. Devou Park's vistas may captivate the eye, but its history demands deeper reflection. How many picnickers and hikers pause to consider the lives of the people who toiled here, their names etched faintly in records but vividly in the soul of the land?

This is why I write—to uncover these layers, to amplify these voices, and to challenge the sanitized narratives that too often dominate our understanding of history. As we walk these trails, let's remember that every step carries us over stories waiting to be told. Let's honor the lives that shaped this land and ensure that their contributions are never forgotten.

At this point in the narrative, I imagine some of you are thinking, "This is all fascinating, but where do the Devou family come into play?" Let's untangle this thread.

After Reverend William Montague's death, I couldn't confirm with absolute certainty who took ownership of the land. My instinct, though, tells me that it likely passed to his children, since they were tasked with the care of Sister Mariah and Brother Armsted in Montague's will. But what I do know is this: by 1860, the land had found its way into the hands of William Devou Sr., a Cincinnati milliner who had amassed enough wealth to purchase vast portions of the Northern Kentucky hillside, including Montague's former property.

Fast-forward a bit, and the spotlight shifts to Devou's sons, William Jr. and Charles, who were instrumental in shaping what we now know as Devou Park. After completing their college studies in Europe—a detail that underscores the family's affluence—the brothers returned home to the greater Cincinnati area. Brief stints in their father's millinery business followed, but it was William Jr. who took a markedly different path, diving headfirst into property acquisition.

William Jr. focused much of his efforts on Cincinnati's West End neighborhood. He had a unique approach to wealth-building; instead of selling the properties he acquired, he reinvested rental profits so he could buy even more. His strategy was deliberate and profitable. Day by day, week by week, month by month, his fortune grew as he leased out his ever-expanding portfolio.

And this is where my "spidey senses" start to tingle. The early 1900s—when William Jr. was on his property-buying spree—coincided with a pivotal chapter in the history of Cincinnati's West End neighborhood, a predominantly Black community at the time. This revelation brought me back to everything I've learned about the West End, its history, and the systemic dynamics at play during this period.

What was really going on here? What forces were shaping this community, and how did William Jr.'s business dealings fit into the larger narrative of race, economics, and power in the city? These are the kinds of questions that make the past come alive for me and remind me why it's so vital to examine history from every angle.

With these layers of history and intrigue, the story of the Devou family deepens, revealing more than just a legacy of land and wealth. It becomes a window into the intersections of privilege, enterprise, and the lived experiences of those whose stories often go untold.

The story of Cincinnati's West End neighborhood is almost as old as the city itself, its history entwined with the pulse of urban growth and the currents of migration that shaped it. To understand its evolution, we need to travel back to a time when the city's ingenuity was on full display, a time of grand engineering feats and transformative transportation networks.

Devou Estate. *Kenton County Public Library.*

Picture this: the completion of Cincinnati's famed inclined planes and the establishment of its electric trolley car system. These marvels of innovation revolutionized mobility, making it easier than ever for people to traverse the city's hilly terrain and reach new horizons beyond the downtown basin. The result? A population explosion and an economic boom that rippled through the area.

Among those drawn to this promise of opportunity were thousands of Black Americans who were seeking to carve out new lives amid the city's rapid expansion. According to a June 2024 post on The Voice of Black Cincinnati, an online resource designed to educate, recognize, and create opportunities for Black Americans in the region, by 1860, the Black population in Cincinnati had swelled to an impressive 3,600, a dramatic leap from the modest figure of just 700 recorded a mere forty years prior.[1] This growth was no mere coincidence. It was the product of hope, resilience, and the pursuit of something better, fueled by the opportunities this burgeoning metropolis seemed to offer.

Amid the neighborhood's vibrant streets and storied landmarks stood Union Baptist Church, a beacon of faith and liberation. Founded in 1831 by fourteen members who faced discrimination in a predominantly white congregation, the church became a sanctuary for Black Cincinnatians seeking community and spiritual guidance. Initially meeting in one member's home, the congregation built their first church in 1835, right here in the West End. During the era of the Underground Railroad, Union Baptist Church stood as a refuge, opening its doors to enslaved people seeking freedom. Its legacy is one of courage, compassion, and an unwavering commitment to justice.

The story of Cincinnati's West End begins with migration—families leaving the South, drawn by the prospect of opportunity in the bustling, growing city. Many of these newcomers settled just beyond the central business district in a neighborhood that would come to be known as the West End.

The West End became a cornerstone of this migration story, a vibrant neighborhood that bore witness to the challenges and triumphs of its residents. This was more than just a shift in numbers; it was a transformation that would leave an indelible mark on Cincinnati's cultural and social fabric. Every brick laid, every streetcar built, and every story lived in the West End during this time contributed to the layered history of a city on the rise.

At the West End's heart was Linn Street, a bustling thoroughfare that connected the neighborhood to the greater city. It was more than just a road; it was a lifeline, tying together the intricate network of streets that made

Top: The Pastors of Union Baptist Church. The congregation was formed in 1831 by fourteen members who had been discriminated against at a predominantly white congregation. Members began meeting in one of their homes until they finished construction of a formal church building in 1835 in the West End. The church was instrumental in helping enslaved people seek refuge along the Underground Railroad. *Robert O'Neal Multicultural Center (ROMAC), Black Cincinnati History Collection.*

Bottom: Kenyon Barr, a notable portion of Cincinnati's West End neighborhood, was completely torn down in the late 1950s as part of what was then called an "urban renewal project." *Cincinnati History Library and Archive, the Cincinnati Museum Center.*

The Tigers, the first Cincinnati Negro League Baseball Team. *Cincinnati Reds Hall of Fame and Museum.*

up the Dayton Street Historic District. This area, with its distinct German townhomes, stood as a testament to the West End's nineteenth-century roots. The ornate façades reflected an era when beer brewers and pork packers called these streets home, their industries shaping not only the neighborhood but also the identity of Cincinnati itself.

In the shadow of these homes stood Crosley Field, a landmark that became synonymous with the spirit of the West End. From 1912 to 1970, it served as the home of the Cincinnati Reds, drawing crowds to its unique V-shaped stadium, affectionately known as the "Old Boomerang." Before it carried the Crosley name, a nod to team owner Powel Crosley Jr., it was simply Redland Field. Yet there was nothing simple about the memories made there. Crosley Field was more than a ballpark; it was a gathering space where the city came together, united in their love for the game and the team that called it home.

William Jr. held properties scattered across the city, but his true empire lay in Cincinnati's West End in the Eighth Ward, as it was then known, though most recognized it as the city's red-light district. At its height, this stretch of shadowed streets and whispered transactions boasted as many as 70 brothels housing close to 700 sex workers. George Street was the spine of it all, with Sixth and Longworth Streets threading through, running between Plum and John Streets like veins feeding the city's unspoken economy. And at the center of it—his domain—William Jr. controlled nearly 120 properties, each one a brick in the foundation of his real estate dynasty.

But beyond the business of bodies and back rooms, the West End pulsed with a rhythm all its own. Jazz spilled from doorways, folding into the night air, mingling with raucous laughter, murmured propositions, and the quiet defiance of those who refused to live within the lines. After dark, the Cotton Club reigned, a smoky, electric sanctuary where the city's only integrated stage made room for the raw brilliance of Black queer performers. Just a few blocks away, the Cordelia Hotel stood in whispered legend, a place where men seeking men and trans women found solace in the flickering haze of gaslight and gin. To outsiders, it was a brothel. But to those who understood its walls intimately, it was something more, a refuge, a secret, a necessary sin in a world too narrow to hold them.

Under the hot, amber glow of the Cotton Club's stage lights, Fajor moved with a hypnotic rhythm, a vision of glamour draped in sequins and smoke. In the roaring nights of early twentieth-century Cincinnati, when jazz pulsed through the veins of the city and Prohibition pushed nightlife into the shadows, Fajor was more than an exotic dancer—he was a spectacle, a mystery, and a legend in the making.

Historians, constrained by the language of their time, deemed Fajor "sissified," a term that, while derogatory by modern standards, hints at the effeminate charm and gender-defying artistry that made them unforgettable. But to those who knew, who watched with rapt attention as they commanded the floor, Fajor was bold, unapologetic, and electric, their name whispered in admiration among those who understood that Cincinnati's West End pulsed with a vibrant, underground queer culture long before the world was ready to embrace it.

The West End of Cincinnati is often remembered for its jazz halls and cultural vibrancy, but beneath that romanticized history lies a hidden world of Black queer life. Jacob Hogue, the author of *Cincinnati Before Stonewall: Untold Queer History of the Queen City*, sheds light on the figures who carved out space for themselves in an era that sought to erase them. Hogue explains:

> *Charlie Howard ruled 514 Smith Street as his own, while Lizzie Irvin, a trans woman, called 604 West Fourth Street home in 1909. The Sterling Hotel at Sixth and Mound became a gathering place, a refuge where whispered stories and forbidden romances unfolded. Solomon Millcreek found his place on West Ninth Street, each address marking a life lived in quiet defiance. And then there was Fajor. More than just a performer, they were a statement—a high-kicking, shimmering refusal to be anything less than extraordinary. History may have reduced them to a footnote, but the glow of the Cotton Club's lights still lingers. And somewhere, in that memory, Fajor still dances.*

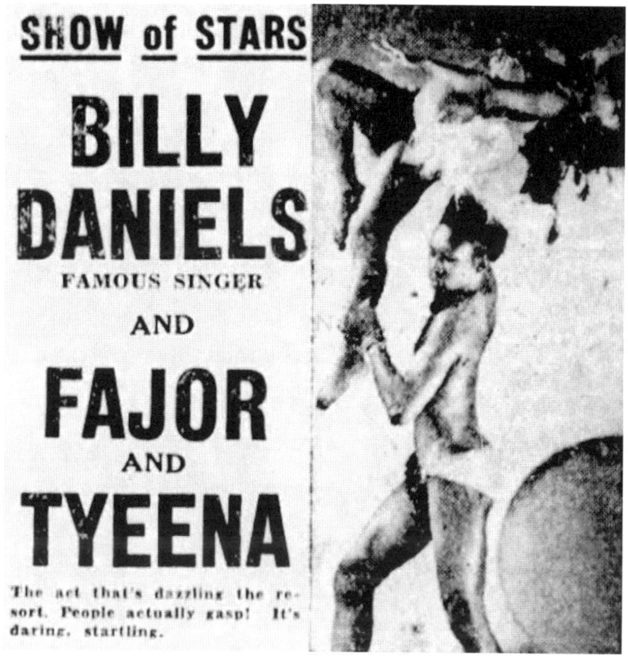

Fajor, the "sissified" exotic dancer who performed at the Cotton Club. *Press of Atlantic City.*

While others sought to define themselves through art and resistance, William Jr. had only one pursuit: wealth. His world was measured in rent payments and land deeds, his fortune growing with each transaction. He slept on a cot in the back of his George Street office, next door to a brothel, cooking his own meals and refusing to hire a single worker. Every repair, every maintenance job he did himself, an exhausting feat for a man who owned more properties than he could count. But William Jr. wasn't one to rely on others. Profit was his gospel, and every boarded-up window, every crumbling brick, was just another step toward more.

Following the death of his mother and father in 1910 and 1897, respectively, William Jr. was named the executor of their vast estate, which included the aforementioned Covington hillside that overlooks the Ohio River, but it was with his brother Charles that he made the decision to donate a large patch of family property—250 parcels that later became Devou Park, valued at just under $1 million—to the City of Covington.

After William Jr.'s death in 1937, the profit from his vast real estate holdings was bequeathed to Covington to be expended on the maintenance and upkeep of Devou Park.

Since 2020, we have seen countless additional challenges to addressing social inequality, with particular notice given to the Black Lives Matter

Movement, which has reignited discussions about systemic racism. In addition, the COVID-19 pandemic has triggered a historic economic downturn, leaving millions wanting and disproportionately affecting the Black community both nationwide and locally. The list of social issues in the United States today can seem overwhelming. With that being said, it is important to recognize that many of the benefits we as a greater Cincinnati community enjoy today came from the generosity of not only prominent families but also the marginalized communities of the past.

To truly honor this legacy, we must confront these intertwined stories, recognizing both the triumphs and inequities that define our shared past.

2

Cincinnati's Taft Museum of Art and Black American Artist Robert S. Duncanson

One of the joys of living in a city as old as Cincinnati is that history doesn't just live in books; it greets you around every corner. There's something almost magical about seeing the layers of time unfold in front of you. Think about it: Cincinnati was founded in 1788, decades before cities like Kansas City, Missouri, even existed. Here, the past isn't just a whisper; it's a shout, echoing through coal-burning furnaces, the remnants of incline planes, and trolley tracks that tell the story of a city conquering its hills. You don't just imagine the ingenuity of yesteryear; you see its bones still standing.

In 2017, I stepped into the living heartbeat of history when I began working at the Taft Museum of Art in downtown Cincinnati. But this wasn't just any museum. No, this was a wooden house standing tall in a city built of brick and stone, a survivor from the early 1800s. The place felt less like a building and more like a time capsule. Its walls had absorbed centuries of change, and every creak of the floorboards seemed eager to spill a secret. I was listening closely.

That's when Anna Sinton Taft enters the story. She may not carry the name recognition of her brother-in-law, President William Howard Taft, but make no mistake, she was a force in her own right, a quiet titan of Cincinnati's art scene. The mansion she called home—what we now know as the Taft Museum—once stood as a crown jewel at the edge of downtown. Yet what makes the space iconic isn't just Anna's presence; it's the layered stories the house still holds, stretching back before her time and echoing long after.

Cincinnati from Mt. Adams, circa 1909, glass plate negatives in the Detroit Publishing Company photograph collection. *Library of Congress, Taft Museum of Art.*

Anna wasn't just a wealthy woman of her era; she was a cultural powerhouse who left her fingerprints all over Cincinnati's arts landscape. And while the house's grandeur spoke volumes about her status, it's the layers of history beneath that opulence that truly captivate. This was a home where art and culture blossomed, where connections to the world beyond Cincinnati's borders thrived, and where the past refused to be forgotten.

The Taft Museum stands firm as a living witness to Cincinnati's unfolding story. From its nineteenth-century roots to its role today as a gathering place for art and history, the house itself reminds us why preservation matters. I've had the privilege of walking those halls, of listening to the echoes tucked within its walls, and what I've come to realize is this: Anna Sinton Taft's legacy isn't confined to the paintings or the sculptures. It pulses through the very bones of the house, woven into the cultural heartbeat of this city.

In 1927, Anna Sinton Taft and her husband, Charles, did something that would forever change Cincinnati's artistic landscape: they bequeathed their grand home and personal art collection to the people of the city. Imagine that—a mansion filled with priceless works of art gifted to a community. After a bit of remodeling and sprucing up, this historic gem reopened in 1932 as the Taft Museum of Art. Today, it's not just a museum; it's a resource, a muse, and, according to a 1999 *UC Magazine* article, it has served as a pseudo classroom, where faculty from the University of Cincinnati's College of Design, Architecture, Art, and Planning still draw inspiration.[2]

But let's talk about how Anna and Charles weren't just stopping at art donations; they were innovators in philanthropy. Their generous endowment sparked something extraordinary: the creation of the nation's very first arts

View of the Tafts' hallway in what is now the Taft Museum of Art, about 1925. *Taft Museum of Art Archives.*

giving organization, a concept so ahead of its time that it still thrives today. The Tafts' bequest was matched by $1 million from the City of Cincinnati, laying the foundation for what became the Cincinnati Institute of Fine Arts.[3] Fast-forward to today, and that organization has evolved into ArtsWave, a powerhouse that fuels hundreds of arts projects and organizations across the greater Cincinnati region through impact-driven grants.

And if you're flipping through the list of National Historic Landmarks, you'll find the Taft Museum proudly among them. But here's why it's on my list of Cincinnati's great places. It's not just about its official status or its significance to the arts community. No, it's about the walls, specifically the walls of the home's foyer, where several original paintings still reside. These aren't just decorations; they're living connections to Anna's vision, a tangible reminder of how she and Charles shaped Cincinnati into a cultural hub.

Standing in that foyer, with history echoing through the walls and timeless art alive all around you, it becomes clear that Anna Sinton Taft wanted to leave behind more than just a house or a collection. He wanted to leave a living legacy. One that still inspires, still uplifts, and still pushes Cincinnati's art scene beyond greatness into something truly transformative.

How did such world-class pieces of art nearly vanish into obscurity, lost to time and indifference? It's a question that beckons us to dig deeper, to unearth the layers of history, intent, and passion that brought these murals into existence. In this chapter, we'll unravel that mystery by peeling back the story of their near loss and miraculous preservation. But that's only the beginning. We'll also explore the visionaries who brought these works to life, the artist whose hands and heart transformed walls into windows of cultural significance, and the local arts organization that has redefined how we see diversity, equity, and inclusion not just in Cincinnati but on a global scale.

Together, we'll trace how the intersection of art, advocacy, and community ignited a movement that transcends paint and canvas, creating a legacy that continues to inspire and transform. Buckle up, because this story isn't just about art; it's about the power of humanity to preserve and uplift the voices that truly matter.

J.P. Ball: A Story of Resilience

For Cincinnati's Black residents, especially earlier in the city's history, the so-called promised land often proved to be an illusion. While the city experienced significant growth with the construction of new roads and the introduction of an electric trolley system during this time, the benefits of progress were not shared equally. By the 1850s, Cincinnati boasted a population of approximately 115,000, making it the sixth-largest city in the

United States. Yet the Black population, numbering just over 3,200, faced entrenched discrimination and limited freedoms, even within the borders of a free state. Their struggles highlighted the chasm between the ideals of liberty and the realities of systemic exclusion.

The mid-nineteenth century was a time of upheaval, with events like the Civil War and the introduction of the Emancipation Proclamation reshaping the nation's identity. In Cincinnati, however, these seismic shifts were accompanied by fear and resistance among white residents. Many viewed free Black communities as a threat to the social and economic order, creating a volatile and often dangerous environment. Despite these challenges, a remarkable number of Black artists in Cincinnati managed to carve out spaces for themselves, achieving recognition and success that defied the odds. Their resilience and creativity shone brightly against the backdrop of a society that often sought to dim their light.

Among these artists was James Presley Ball, better known as J.P. Ball, a pioneering Black daguerreotypist and photographer. Born in Virginia in 1825, Ball moved to Cincinnati in the 1840s and opened one of the most celebrated photography studios of his time. His studio, Ball's Great Daguerrean Gallery of the West, became a cultural hub, attracting clients from all walks of life, including abolitionists, politicians, and members of

J.P. Ball, portrait of an unidentified child, 1858–60, ninth plate daguerreotype with applied color, half-cased. *Smithsonian American Art Museum, the L.J. West Collection of Early African American Photography.*

the city's elite. Ball's work not only showcased his technical mastery but also served as a powerful form of representation, capturing the dignity and humanity of Black Americans during a time when such images were scarce.

Ball's contributions extended beyond photography. He was an outspoken abolitionist and used his art to challenge the institution of slavery. His detailed panoramic painting *Mammoth Pictorial Tour of the United States Comprising Views of the African Slave Trade* was a bold statement against slavery, illustrating its horrors and injustices. This work toured extensively and was a testament to Ball's commitment to social justice, blending artistry with activism.

The barriers artists like Ball faced were immense. While Ohio's 1802 constitution outlawed slavery, the enactment of the Black Laws in 1804 and 1807 made it abundantly clear that freedom in name did not equate to equality. These laws imposed severe restrictions on Black Americans, curtailing their rights to move freely, access certain jobs, and participate fully in civic life. This legal framework set the tone for Cincinnati's treatment of its Black population, fostering an atmosphere of hostility and exclusion.

By the late 1820s, tensions in the city had reached a boiling point. In 1829, a violent race riot erupted when a white mob targeted Black workers for simply walking down the street. The growing Black population, combined with the perception that Black Americans were competing for jobs, particularly in the working-class sectors, incited fear and anger among white laborers. This riot was not an isolated incident but part of a larger pattern of racial violence. In 1841, another riot broke out when Irish dockworkers attacked Black residents, leaving fifty-six people dead and injuring over two hundred. Such acts of violence, often fueled by economic anxiety and racial prejudice, became a recurring theme throughout the 1840s, further marginalizing the Black community.

Yet amid this turmoil, Cincinnati's Black residents refused to be defined by their circumstances. Education became a central pillar of their resistance and empowerment. Despite being segregated and underfunded, Black schools in Cincinnati offered more than just academic instruction; they served as hubs for political and social activism. These schools became places where the seeds of progress were sown, nurturing a generation of leaders who would go on to challenge the status quo. One notable institution was the private, all-Black Gilmore High School for Negroes. Its graduates included figures like John I. Gaines, a dedicated abolitionist, and Peter H. Clark, a trailblazing politician, educator, and community activist. Their accomplishments underscored the transformative power of education in a society that sought to deny them opportunities.

Portrait of J.P. Ball. *From the* Cincinnati Enquirer.

For Black artists like J.P. Ball, the challenges were no less daunting. The racially charged environment made it difficult to secure patrons or institutional support, yet Ball's studio thrived, becoming a beacon of Black excellence and innovation. His ability to navigate these challenges and produce work that resonated across racial and social boundaries speaks to the strength and ingenuity of Cincinnati's Black community.

Cincinnati's Black artists, educators, and activists played pivotal roles in shaping the city's identity, even as they faced systemic barriers and routine violence. Figures like J.P. Ball not only elevated the cultural landscape of the city but also left a lasting legacy of resistance and creativity. Their stories remind us that progress is often born from struggle and that art and education remain powerful tools for challenging oppression. Together, they built a foundation for future generations to continue the fight for equity and recognition, making their contributions an enduring part of Cincinnati's history.

Nicholas Longworth and Robert S. Duncanson

Nicholas Longworth's story is one of transformation, a journey from the grips of poverty to becoming one of the wealthiest men in America. Arriving in Cincinnati in 1803 from the farmlands of New Jersey, he came seeking opportunity and wealth. By the time of his passing in 1863, Longworth had amassed an estimated fortune of $20 million, cementing his legacy as not just a celebrated wine merchant but also one of the most influential figures of his era. His tax bill alone, at one point second only to John Jacob Astor's, spoke volumes about his financial success. Beyond his wealth, Longworth was a patron of the arts, shaping the cultural fabric of Cincinnati. He even called home a grand residence that later became the Taft Museum of Art, a living testament to his influence and a space where art and history converge.

In the same city, though worlds apart in status, a Black painter by the name of Robert S. Duncanson was leaving his own mark. Originally from

Upstate New York, Duncanson was one of seven siblings and the son of a house painter whose craft adorned the interiors of homes. Yet Duncanson's vision extended far beyond walls; his art captured landscapes and narratives that defied the constraints placed on Black artistry in a nation grappling with its identity.

Together, their stories reflect the complex interplay of wealth, creativity, and social justice in nineteenth-century Cincinnati, a city bustling with ambition, contradictions, and the pursuit of lasting legacies.

The Duncanson Murals

Robert S. Duncanson's eight murals in what is now the Taft Museum of Art are more than decorative achievements; they are testaments to his mastery and resilience. Art historian Joseph D. Ketner II once described these works as "the most accomplished domestic mural paintings in America before the Civil War." Yet like the artist, who painstakingly devoted two years to their creation, mixing each hue by hand, these murals faded from public memory, papered over by the Longworth family before Duncanson's death.

It's a cruel irony that art of such magnitude, produced by a Black man in a time when society sought to suppress his every contribution, could be so easily dismissed. But perhaps that's the way history often treats Black brilliance: celebrated in fleeting moments and then buried until it is rediscovered by those willing to unearth its significance. Duncanson's murals, with their

View of the Longworth Foyer in the present day. *Taft Museum of Art.*

William Notman, portrait of Robert S. Duncanson, 1864. *Notman Photographic Archives, McCord Museum, McGill University, Montreal; Taft Museum of Art.*

intricate detail and illusionistic grandeur, speak to not only his technical skill but also his persistence in claiming space where few believed he belonged.

In 1861, the *Daily Cincinnati Gazette* hailed Robert S. Duncanson as "the best landscape painter in the West," and the Smithsonian American Art Museum later lauded him as "perhaps the most accomplished Black American painter in the United States from 1850 to 1860."[4] Such acclaim wasn't mere hyperbole; it was a reflection of Duncanson's extraordinary talent

Robert S. Duncanson (American, 1821–1872), landscape mural, 1850–52, oil on painted plaster. *Bequest of Charles Phelps Taft and Anna Sinton Taft, 1932.238; Taft Museum of Art.*

and vision. Duncanson's art was—and remains—a profound statement of resilience and creativity in a time when the odds were stacked against him.

So, when those long-forgotten murals emerged from behind layers of wallpaper in 1930 and later, in 2004, were given new life through meticulous restoration, it felt as though destiny was stepping back into the light. Today, these sweeping landscapes decorate the Taft Museum of Art bearing witness to a legacy that refused silence. Once overlooked and now guarded with care and celebrated by a city that nearly missed their worth, the murals stand as unshakable proof of Duncanson's genius and the undeniable endurance of Black artistry.

Robert S. Duncanson's journey from a humble interior painter to a celebrated artist is a story of persistence, self-determination, and vision. Initially earning his living painting walls and portraits, Duncanson secured his legacy through not only his breathtaking landscape murals but also the Belmont Murals and the Taft Museum of Art's Duncanson Artist-in-Residence Program. Since its inception in 1986, this program has honored outstanding artists across disciplines—painters, photographers, musicians, dancers, authors, and poets—from Cincinnati and across the nation, keeping Duncanson's spirit alive and inspiring new generations of creatives.

Though details about his early years are sparse, historians believe that when Duncanson was around ten years old, his family relocated to Michigan. It was likely there, amid the natural beauty of the Hudson River and its surroundings, that his love for landscapes was born. His early exposure to these scenes profoundly shaped the style he later refined and brought to life in his murals. In Michigan, Duncanson also got his start as a businessman, working alongside his father in the family's interior painting trade.

Duncanson's entrepreneurial spirit shines through in the way he marketed himself, placing advertisements in local papers to attract clients—a nineteenth-century parallel to today's websites and social media campaigns. Meanwhile, he poured his energy into self-teaching the art of landscape painting. He balanced his nine-to-five work as a portrait painter with a dedication to perfecting his craft, exhibiting his works wherever he could and building his reputation step by step.

In 1840, Duncanson moved to Cincinnati, a city where his talent and ambition could flourish. It was here that he transitioned from painting portraits to producing the grand landscape murals that would define his legacy. Cincinnati, with its vibrant artistic community, offered him the platform to grow as an artist while continuing to hone his skills.

Interestingly, Duncanson's work can be found just across the river in Covington, Kentucky. The Baker Hunt Art and Cultural Center holds a rare Duncanson portrait in its collection. If you ever have the chance to visit, be sure to ask a docent to show it to you; it's a piece of history that connects our local story to his larger-than-life legacy.

Duncanson's story is more than a tale of artistic success. It's a reminder that creativity, when paired with persistence and resourcefulness, can transcend boundaries and leave an indelible mark on history.

Cincinnati in the mid-nineteenth century was fertile ground for an ambitious artist like Robert S. Duncanson. The city was home to the first art academy in the Midwest and boasted a thriving cultural scene, offering unmatched opportunities for artists to grow and thrive. Duncanson made his debut in this dynamic environment during the Society for the Promotion of Useful Knowledge exhibition in 1842, showcasing two works: *Infant Savior* and *A Fancy Portrait*. Critics of the time, however, singled out his portrait of William J. Baker as the most impressive portrait of this early period, a testament to his emerging skill and artistry.

Yet Duncanson's true calling was still ahead of him. About a decade after arriving in Cincinnati, he turned his focus fully to landscape painting. His move to Mount Pleasant, a community of abolitionists and free Black men later renamed Mount Healthy, marked a pivotal moment in his journey. Surrounded by like-minded individuals advocating for freedom and equality, Duncanson found both personal and artistic inspiration.

He honed his craft by studying prints and experimenting with photography, a medium still in its infancy. These experiences informed his technique and broadened his creative vision. By 1852, Duncanson began exhibiting landscapes influenced by the Hudson River School, a style characterized by its romantic, detailed depictions of nature's grandeur.[5] This shift not only marked a new chapter in his career but also solidified his reputation as one of the most significant landscape artists of his time.

Cincinnati may have been a complex and often unwelcoming place for a Black man in the nineteenth century, but for Duncanson, it provided the resources, connections, and community he needed to cultivate his craft. His move to Mount Pleasant wasn't just geographic; it was symbolic, a step toward building a life and legacy grounded in freedom, creativity, and self-expression.

DUNCANSON ALSO WAS AN ABOLITIONIST

Robert S. Duncanson, like many prominent Black Americans of his time, used his artistry and influence to further the cause of abolition. Navigating the delicate and often treacherous divide between Cincinnati's Black and white societies in the mid-1800s, Duncanson leveraged his light brown complexion and charisma to move seamlessly between the two worlds. This ability wasn't just about access; it was a calculated tool he wielded in the fight against slavery.

In 1855, when J.P. Ball, as noted previously, the celebrated Black photographer and abolitionist, assembled the nation's first collective of Black artists, he turned to Duncanson. The project—a staggering 2,500-square-yard mural exposing the horrors of slavery—was an ambitious and harrowing

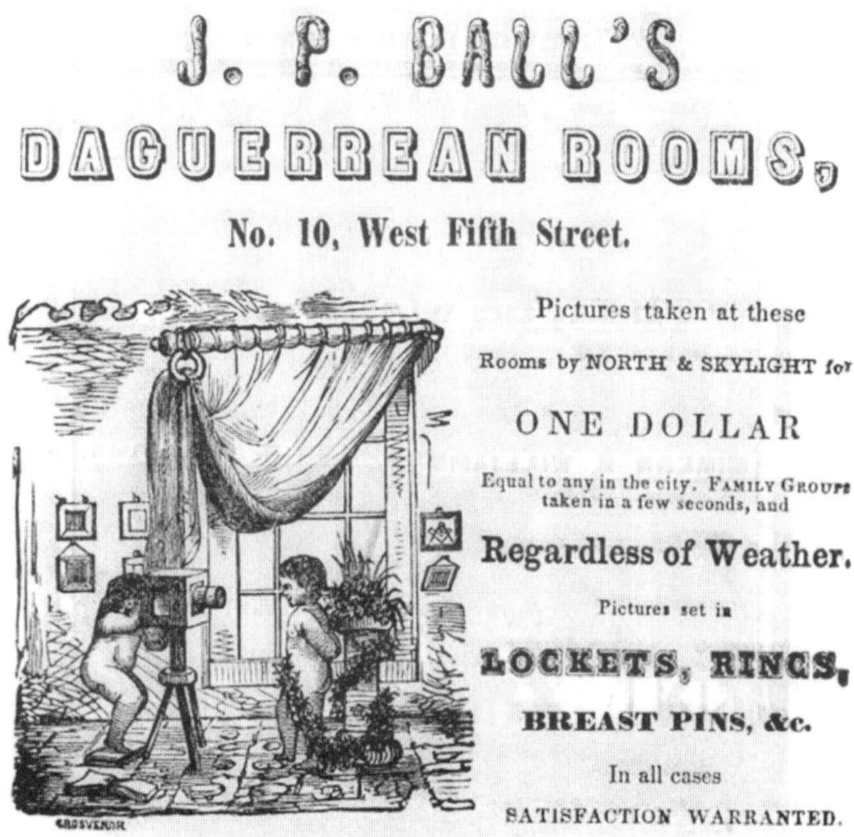

Illustrated J.P. Ball advertisement. *Cincinnati Museum Center.*

endeavor. Duncanson served as both advisor and touch-up artist, lending his talent to ensure the mural delivered its powerful message with precision and impact.

It was during this period that Duncanson also caught the attention of Nicholas Longworth.

Through these connections and collaborations, Duncanson not only advanced his artistic career but also embedded his work within the broader struggle for freedom and equality. His ability to navigate Cincinnati's social complexities, coupled with his unwavering commitment to abolition, positioned him as both a masterful artist and an advocate for change. His legacy is a reminder that art, in the right hands, can be as much a tool of liberation as it is of beauty.

Robert S. Duncanson's big break came in 1850, when Nicholas Longworth commissioned him to paint murals in the entry hall of Belmont, the Longworth family's grand estate—what we now know as the Taft Museum of Art. This opportunity wasn't just a job; it was an introduction to a world of patronage and prestige that would elevate Duncanson's career to new heights.

Some might argue that Duncanson's acceptance into wealthy white homes was made easier by his lighter complexion, a byproduct of his complex heritage. His great-grandfather, a Scottish slaveholder in Virginia, fathered a child with an enslaved woman, and that son—Duncanson's grandfather—became the plantation's house painter. Through his trade, Duncanson's grandfather earned enough money to buy his freedom and move his family north, setting the stage for Robert's eventual rise.[6]

Yes, Duncanson was Black. Yes, he painted murals for a rich white man. But to reduce his success to these facts alone is to miss the full measure of his ambition and genius. Robert S. Duncanson wasn't just painting walls; he was crafting a legacy. By the 1860s, he was celebrated nationwide as the "best landscape painter in the West." (Remember, back then, the Midwest was the nation's western frontier.) His reputation extended beyond America's borders, with newspapers in London praising him as a peer to British contemporaries.

Duncanson's work stood shoulder to shoulder with the greats of his era, artists like Thomas Cole, Asher Brown Durand, and John Frederick Kensett, who defined the Hudson River School's landscape tradition.[7] His ability to rival these luminaries, despite the odds stacked against him as a Black artist in a racially divided America, is a testament to his skill, determination, and vision. Duncanson didn't just aspire to greatness; he achieved it, carving a place for himself in the annals of American art history.

Not long after his big break, Robert Duncanson seemed to vanish from Cincinnati for a time—a move some historians believe was deliberate. The theory is that Duncanson, concerned about the racial tensions of his environment and seeking creative freedom, journeyed north to Canada before making his way to Europe. And in Europe? Well, let's just say he wasn't just another painter—he was a sensation. Duncanson rubbed elbows with earls, duchesses, and even the king of Sweden, who personally purchased his acclaimed painting *Land of the Lotus Eaters*. There's even speculation that Queen Victoria herself acquired one of his works. Looks like Duncanson was ahead of his time, setting the stage for future trailblazers like Josephine Baker and James Baldwin to discover the allure of Europe's more inclusive artistic circles.

The late 1860s marked the pinnacle of Duncanson's career as a landscape artist. He opened a gallery in Cincinnati, producing masterpiece after masterpiece, including evocative views of the Scottish Highlands that reflected his ancestral roots. His work toured the nation, fetching prices as high as $15,000—equivalent to around $300,000 today. Imagine that: a Black man, in the mid-nineteenth century, commanding such prices and respect for his art.

But even the brightest flames eventually fade. Robert S. Duncanson passed away in October 1872, leaving behind a legacy as vast as the landscapes he painted. He was laid to rest in his boyhood home of Monroe, Michigan, and his work continues to ensure that his name is etched permanently into the story of American art. Duncanson painted his way into immortality, proving that no boundary—geographical, societal, or otherwise—could limit his brilliance.

Robert Duncanson's Legacy

The incredible news is that Robert Duncanson's legacy is as vibrant today as the colors he meticulously blended over a century and a half ago. His legendary set of eight framed murals, commissioned for what was then the Longworth home and is now the Taft Museum of Art, remain at the forefront of discussions about American art history. Crafted over the course of a nearly two-year renovation, these murals are widely celebrated as some of the most accomplished domestic artworks in pre–Civil War America, an enduring testament to Duncanson's unmatched skill and vision.

Here's the twist of fate: these masterpieces almost disappeared forever. They were hidden beneath layers of wallpaper until Anna Sinton, a subsequent owner of the home, reportedly made a final, fervent plea—some say on her deathbed—for someone to investigate the foyer walls. She had heard whispers over the years about paintings concealed there, and thankfully, she trusted those rumors.

And let me just say—thank goodness she did.

What emerged from beneath the wallpaper wasn't just art; it was a revelation. These murals became the cornerstone of Duncanson's enduring legacy, a legacy that has only grown richer with time. Today, his impact extends beyond the walls of the Taft Museum. In 1986, the museum launched the Duncanson Artist-in-Residence Program, a transformative initiative honoring the creative contributions of Black American artists across disciplines.

So, when you step into the Taft Museum of Art, you're entering a living dialogue between history, resilience, and artistry. Here, Duncanson's legacy does more than endure; it breathes, it flourishes, and it continues to challenge and inspire new generations of artists to imagine boldly and reach beyond limits.

3

Cincinnati's Union Terminal and the Black Elks of Northern Kentucky

Growing up in the '80s and '90s, I was a closeted history buff, especially when it came to local history. But I didn't just want to learn about the history that was most often told, the history that filled my grade school textbooks, centered on white narratives. That history was mine, too, but I craved more. I wanted to know about my history, about the Black stories woven into the same streets and spaces I called home. So, every chance I got, I searched for it, gathering fragments of our past like puzzle pieces, trying to see the fuller picture of where I came from.

But on Saturdays? Saturdays belonged to something else entirely.

In our house, the most sacred fixture in the living room wasn't the couch, the coffee table, or even the family photos on the wall—it was the television. And in the world before streaming services—before you could pull up any show at any time—Saturday mornings were all about event television. There was no on-demand, no skipping commercials, no binge-watching. It was all about waking up early, pouring a bowl of cereal (mine was Total, though most of my friends were loyal to Frosted Flakes or Cap'n Crunch), and planting myself in front of the screen for hours while my mom enjoyed a little extra sleep.

For an entire generation of kids who grew up in the 1980s, Saturday morning cartoons were it. The countdown to the weekend was just as much about that sacred block of programming as it was about a break from school. And for me, there was one show that reigned supreme: *Super Friends*.

Superman. Batman. Wonder Woman. Aquaman. The Wonder Twins. All stationed at the legendary Hall of Justice, working together to save the world, week after week. But what made *Super Friends* even more fascinating? Its connection to my own backyard.

The Hall of Justice—its towering, futuristic structure—wasn't just some random design pulled from the creative ether. It was inspired by the Cincinnati Union Terminal, a landmark right here in my city. And Hanna-Barbera, the animation powerhouse behind the show, had roots in Cincinnati, too.

I had spent so much time searching for traces of my history in local spaces, and yet, without even realizing it, a piece of that history had been hiding in plain sight on my television screen every Saturday morning.

Cincinnati Union Terminal

Cincinnati Union Terminal has always held a special place in my heart—not just because its grand silhouette inspired the Hall of Justice in *Super Friends*, my favorite Saturday morning escape, but also because it's a monument to a city that has always been at the crossroads of movement, innovation, and artistry.

Born out of the roaring ambition of the 1920s, Union Terminal was designed to do something remarkable—consolidate thirteen rail lines from seven different systems into one grand station. It was a feat of engineering, merging the raw power of the Machine Age with the romance of travel, all while standing as a testament to Cincinnati's deep artistic roots.[8] By the early 1930s, the station was complete, and at its peak, it was a symphony of motion—216 trains passing through daily, half arriving, half departing, each one carrying people, stories, and possibilities.

But history has a way of shifting course.

On a cold December night in 1941, the station bore witness to a turning point in time, one that would be etched into history as the day that lived in infamy. As President Franklin D. Roosevelt addressed the nation, marking America's entry into World War II, Union Terminal saw a sudden, urgent resurgence. Troops flooded through its halls, now bound for distant battlefields rather than weekend getaways. For a brief moment in history, Cincinnati Union Terminal was alive again, pulsing with purpose.

But as quickly as the tide rose, it receded. By the 1950s and '60s, the golden age of rail travel faded, replaced by the growing dominance of the automobile. The open road became the new symbol of freedom, and Union Terminal, once a crown jewel of transit, saw its platforms grow quieter.

Yet, like all icons, it never truly disappeared. The building itself stood resilient, waiting for the day when people would once again look up and recognize the beauty, history, and undeniable presence of one of Cincinnati's most treasured landmarks.

SEGREGATED RAIL TRAVEL

That's why, whenever I step into what is now the Cincinnati Museum Center, Union Terminal's current reincarnation, I can't help but get lost in the echoes of Union Terminal's past. The signs of its former life as a bustling train station are everywhere—if you know where to look. I walk through those grand halls, picturing the hundreds of thousands of people who once passed through, each with their own destination, their own stories. I think about the Black travelers who made their way through this space—some entering through different doors, some confined to certain areas, but all still very much there.

What's fascinating—almost surprising—is that while segregation was law in so many train stations across the country during most of the time the station was in operation, Cincinnati's Union Terminal didn't bear the same scars of enforced separation seen elsewhere. That's not to say it was a haven of equality—far from it. But in an era when Jim Crow ruled nearly every aspect of American life, when even stepping into a station could be a reminder of where you weren't welcome, Cincinnati's terminal functioned with a level of openness that was not often found in places of its size and stature.

Chicago, Illinois; pullman porter at the Union Station. *Library of Congress.*

That didn't mean traveling while Black was easy—not by a long shot.

Long before Black passengers even boarded their trains, humiliation awaited. By the 1890s, the so-called separate but equal laws had already crept into train stations across the South, mandating separate waiting rooms.[9]

And while only a few states—Arkansas, Louisiana, and Mississippi—had officially passed laws requiring segregated facilities before 1899, "colored" waiting rooms were already common. These rooms, built and maintained by the railroads, were often an afterthought, smaller, less comfortable, and less convenient than the accommodations for white passengers. They were reminders, before journeys even began, of one's place in the racial hierarchy of America.

But despite these realities, Black people were essential to the golden age of rail travel.

Enter the Pullman porters.

If you rode a train in the golden age of rail travel, chances are you encountered a Pullman porter, a uniformed Black man who tended to passengers' every need, ensuring their journeys were smooth and comfortable. The Pullman Company exclusively hired Black men for these roles, and while the work was grueling, these porters became the backbone of luxury rail travel. From 1868 to 1968, their presence on American trains was as iconic as the locomotives themselves. By the 1920s, when railroads were at their peak, more than twenty thousand Black men worked as Pullman porters and train personnel, making it the single largest category of Black employment in the United States and Canada at the time.[10]

These porters were more than just workers; they were symbols of perseverance, dignity, and quiet resistance. They carried the weight of a job that demanded excellence but often gave little in return. Yet, through their service, they helped shape the Black middle class, fueling movements for economic empowerment and civil rights.

So, when I walk through Union Terminal today, I don't just see a museum. I see the layers of history, the people who moved through its halls, the stories they carried, the struggles they faced, and the legacies they left behind.

The Black Elks

Cincinnati was a city built for the rhythm of rail travel, and the Pullman porters were right at home here. They didn't just work the trains that rolled in and out of Union Terminal; they lived, built families, and shaped communities across the greater Cincinnati region. And in late 1898, one of those porters, Arthur James Riggs, found himself in conversation with an attorney from Covington, Kentucky, Benjamin Franklin "B.F." Howard.

Benjamin Franklin Howard, or B.F. Howard, founder of the Improved Benevolent Protective Order of Elks of the World, also called the Black Elks. *Kenton County Public Library*.

What started as a chance exchange between two Black men on different professional paths soon became something far greater—one of the largest Black fraternal organizations in the world, which still stands strong today.

"I'm a member of the Improved Benevolent and Protective Order of Elks of the World—or more commonly, the Black Elks," said Ms. Robbie Williams, a current member of IRA Lodge No. 37 in Covington, Kentucky, the very organization founded by Riggs and Howard. The Black Elks were built on a foundation of service, providing charitable aid, scholarships for local students, veteran support, assistance for seniors and at-risk families, and youth programs in Black communities. "It's international…worldwide! We have lodges across the United States and beyond, even in Japan and the Bahamas."

The first Black Elks lodge in Cincinnati found its home at the Masonic Hall on George Street, a space that saw generations of Black leaders come through its doors. Today, Williams serves as the lodge's directress of civil liberties and directress of education while also representing the organization's regional Ohio B.F. Howard Shrine Department.

But the birth of the Black Elks wasn't just a matter of community; it was an act of bold defiance.

Arthur Riggs, a Pullman porter by trade, saw a need for a Black fraternal organization that could serve and uplift the Black community in a time when access to such spaces was severely limited. He looked to the Benevolent and Protective Order of Elks (the Elks), a prominent fraternal order founded in 1868, as a model. And then, one fateful day while working a train, Riggs stumbled on a copy of the Elks' ritual book, handed to him, unknowingly, by a white member.

That moment changed everything.

"Arthur Riggs worked as a Pullman Porter in the late 1800s," Williams explained. "One day, while on the job, he got his hands on a copy of the Elks' ritual. He read it, recognized exactly what it was, and knew right then and there that he wanted to build a Black organization in its image."

Riggs understood the risks. Black-led organizations faced immense scrutiny, particularly in Kentucky, where incorporation laws were wielded as tools to suppress Black economic and social power. So, before making any moves, he consulted a lawyer. And after scouring the Register of Copyrights at the Library of Congress in Washington, D.C., they found something unexpected—the Elks had never officially copyrighted their rituals.

So, Riggs did what any forward-thinking man in his position would do.

He filed for the copyright himself.

That, of course, is when trouble came knocking.

"The only reason the Elks even knew Riggs had a copy of their rituals," Williams says, "was because he tried to copyright them. And when they found out, they found him—tracked him down at work in Birmingham, Alabama, and demanded he return the documents. They didn't just ask. They threatened him and his family, making it clear that if he didn't hand everything back the next day, there would be consequences."

Riggs never showed up for work the next day. Instead, he and his family fled to safety in Springfield, Ohio.

At the turn of the twentieth century, segregation and Jim Crow laws were tightening their grip on the country, especially in the South, where launching a Black fraternal organization was an uphill battle. But Riggs and Howard found inspiration in leaders like Booker T. Washington, who urged Black Americans to build wealth and social capital through vocational training and economic self-sufficiency.

Following Washington's lead, Riggs entrusted the ritual to B.F. Howard, a practicing Black attorney in Covington. Howard took on the legal fight, filing the copyright under his name as a proprietor rather than an author, rearranging sections of the text to strengthen their claim.

Even with these precautions, the newly formed Improved Benevolent and Protective Order of Elks of the World—soon known simply as the Black Elks—was not out of danger.

Before leaving town, Riggs handed over all the trademarked materials to Howard, effectively making Covington, Kentucky, the organization's new headquarters.

And here's the twist: the only thing that truly set the Black Elks apart from the original Elks was a single word, *improved*.

It wasn't just a word. It was a statement.

Riggs and Howard, two Kentuckians born in the shadow of slavery, envisioned something greater for Black people in America. They saw an opportunity to build an institution where Black men could take pride in

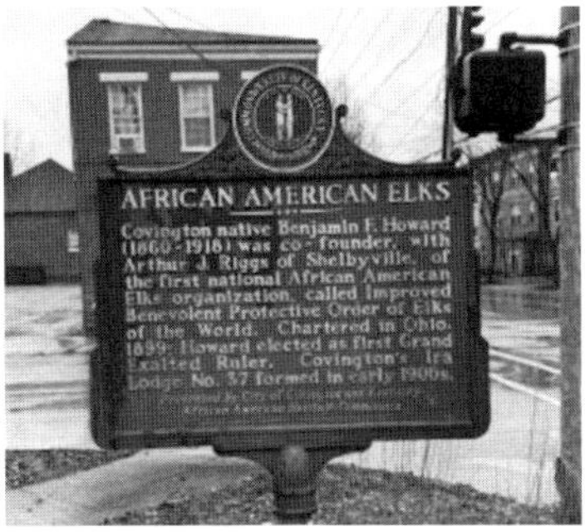

The Black Elks historical marker located in Covington, Kentucky, at the official B.F. Howard Park. *K.A. Simpson Collection.*

themselves, their communities, and the promise of a future they could help shape.

And it worked.

Northern Kentucky's Black community began to flex its collective strength, using organizations like the Black Elks as a foundation for empowerment. Even the *Kentucky Post* took notice, describing B.F. Howard as the "Black Ingersoll," a nod to Robert Green Ingersoll, the renowned lecturer known for his speeches on science, humanism, and social progress.

Despite its rocky start, the Black Elks have not only survived but thrived. Today, the organization boasts over 500,000 members in more than 1,500 lodges worldwide, making it the largest Black fraternal organization in existence.

And Covington hasn't forgotten its native son.

A state historical marker now stands in the median on Eleventh Street between Greenup and Scott Streets, Covington's B.F. Howard Park, honoring B.F. Howard's contributions. It was the twenty-sixth such marker approved by the Kentucky Historical Society for Covington, a city whose history is deeply intertwined with the legacy of Black resilience.

Howard passed away in 1918, but his story—and that of the Black Elks—lives on. His final resting place is Historic Linden Grove Cemetery and Arboretum in Covington, where his legacy continues to whisper through the trees, a reminder of what two men dared to build when the world told them they couldn't.

4

Boss Cox, His Mansion, and Black Cincinnati

I've always been captivated by historic buildings. It doesn't matter if they sit proudly in the heart of a bustling metropolis or stand as forgotten relics in some quiet, rural expanse. Whether meticulously preserved or left to the mercy of time, each one has a story, a pulse, a past worth uncovering. I love wandering through their spaces, peering into the nooks and crannies, imagining the lives that once filled these rooms, and figuring out what made these places matter.

As a kid, my mother attended the University of Cincinnati, and every so often, she had no choice but to take me along for the ride. Childcare was expensive—still is—so I became an unofficial observer of the city's architectural wonders during those trips. The university itself sits at the edge of Clifton, a neighborhood that's long been a mix of Old World grandeur and youthful energy. The southern part bustles with bars, apartments, and restaurants catering to college students, but farther north, the landscape shifts. Here, Cincinnati's elite of the late nineteenth and early twentieth centuries built their mansions, grand homes with sweeping gardens and towering trees, a testament to a time when wealth made itself known in brick, stone, and iron gates.

Clifton itself has deep roots, originally spanning six hundred acres as a farm owned by Charles S. Clarkson, a pork merchant who helped fuel Cincinnati's boom in the 1800s. As the city expanded, the farm gave way to a village in 1850, attracting the who's who of Cincinnati society. Even the fountain that still stands on Clifton Avenue is a remnant of that era, a gift from Henry Probasco, the same man responsible for downtown Cincinnati's iconic Tyler Davidson Fountain. You know the one. If you've ever watched WKRP in Cincinnati, it's there in the opening credits, forever flowing.

But here's what often gets overlooked in the retelling of Cincinnati's past—Black Americans played an undeniable role in shaping this city. Their fight for racial equity, social justice, and economic stability wove into the fabric of Cincinnati's history, even when their contributions were ignored or erased. These truths simmered in my mind, even as a child, especially on those weekly rides to Clifton with my mom. There was one house that always caught my attention. Every trip, I'd beg my mom to drive past it. Something about it called to me, and years later, I would come to know that house intimately, because when I attended the University of Cincinnati, I lived there.

That house? It belonged to none other than George Barnesdale "Boss" Cox, one of Cincinnati's most infamous political kingpins. And, of course, a man like Boss Cox wasn't about to commission just any architect to design his home. He went straight to Hannaford & Sons, the powerhouse firm behind some of Cincinnati's most iconic structures—Cincinnati's City Hall, Music Hall, and over three hundred other buildings across the region. The firm built Boss Cox a mansion in the heart of the Clifton Gaslight District, and let me tell you, stepping inside that house was like stepping into history itself.

From 1895 until his death in 1916, Boss Cox ruled his empire from the home, affectionately called Parkview Manor, entertaining guests lavishly in rooms designed to impress. His wife held onto the home until her passing in 1938, eventually bequeathing it to Union Bethel as a residence for girls until 1947. And then? It took a wild turn—it became a fraternity house for Pi Kappa Alpha.

But no matter how many hands it passed through, the house retained its spirit. Its walls still whispered of power plays and political schemes, of extravagant parties and quiet moments of contemplation. And for me, it became something even more—a personal touchstone, a place where my love for history wasn't just observed but also lived.

Buildings like these aren't just brick and mortar. They are memory. They are legacy. They are the stories waiting to be told.

In 2007, Michael L. Dever made a decision that would forever alter the legacy of this historic property. By 2010, he had donated it to the Public Library of Cincinnati and Hamilton County, setting the stage for its transformation into what we now know as the library system's Clifton Branch. The structure, once worn by time and the echoes of six decades of fraternity brothers, underwent an extensive renovation to meet the demands of a modern public space. When its doors officially reopened on May 28, 2015, it wasn't just a building that had been restored; it was a piece of Cincinnati's history, repurposed for the community.

But who were the Black voices who shaped the world in which Boss Cox lived?

If you're like me, your high school history classes probably skimmed over the leaders who defined the 1800s. The curriculum jumped from the birth of our nation straight into the World Wars, leaving little room for the rich and complex narratives in between, especially those brought by Black and brown faces. It wasn't until I found myself living in this very home as a member of the Alpha Xi chapter of Pi Kappa Alpha that I stumbled on the story of its original owner and his undeniable influence on the city.

Born in Cincinnati in 1853, Cox was the son of British immigrants. His father's early death forced him into the labor force at just eight years old, a fate shared by many poor Cincinnatians of the time. He hustled wherever he could, running errands, shining shoes, working in butcher shops and gambling parlors, and even picking up shifts on the city's bustling steamboats. But Cox wasn't content with just scraping by.[11]

Cincinnati was changing during this period. The city had ballooned into the sixth largest in the United States, and its Black population—though small at 3,200[12]—was a force in its own right. Cox, sharp and ambitious, recognized both the economic opportunity and racial tensions brewing in his West End neighborhood, a place journalist Wendell P. Dabney once dubbed "Dead Man's Corner" due to its gritty underbelly.[13] He saw power in community, influence in numbers, and an opportunity to carve his own path.

With his earnings, Cox bought a saloon in the heart of the West End, embedding himself in one of the largest Black communities in the country at that time. He witnessed firsthand the racial animosity that simmered beneath the surface. Ohio had never legalized slavery, but freedom didn't mean safety. White mobs targeted Black communities in Cincinnati on at least three separate occasions—first in 1829, when an estimated 1,100 Black residents fled to Canada, then again in 1836, and once more in 1841. These weren't isolated incidents; they were violent, organized attacks meant to suppress Black economic and social progress. In one of the most extreme acts of terror, in 1841, a mob wheeled out a cannon and aimed it directly at Bucktown, a Black neighborhood near Sixth Street and Broadway, before being halted by the militia.[14]

Cox wasn't just a businessman; he was a witness to history. He saw power shift, alliances form, and communities rise and fall. And in the shadows of it all, Black Cincinnatians—his neighbors, his patrons, his rivals—were shaping the city's destiny in ways history books rarely acknowledge.

So, I ask again: Who were the Black voices who shaped the world in which this man lived? And why are their stories still fighting to be heard?

Cox didn't earn the nickname "Boss" just because he liked the sound of it. His grip on Cincinnati politics came from his ability to deliver results, especially to the Republican Party. Though he struggled when it came to winning elections himself—losing bids for Hamilton County clerk in both 1884 and 1888—his true power was never meant to be confined to a ballot. Instead, he thrived behind the scenes, orchestrating campaigns, pulling strings, and ensuring that the right people stayed in power.

Take James G. Blaine's 1884 presidential campaign, for instance. Cox ran the Hamilton County operation, establishing the Young Men's Blaine Club as his political nerve center. From there, he cleaned up local conventions, cracked down on fraudulent voting practices (at least the ones he didn't benefit from), and championed reform-minded business candidates for mayor, most of whom won. Under his coalition, Cincinnati politics shifted. Some say it was changed for the better. His machine, as the history books tell it, "brought positive government to Cincinnati" and tamed the chaos of a rapidly expanding city. But at what cost?

Cox built his empire on the struggles of everyday Cincinnatians, and early in his rise, he found an unlikely political ally in the Black community. Maybe it was the shared story of hardship, though it's hard to equate the struggles of a poor white family to that of a poor Black family in nineteenth-century America. Still, he positioned himself as someone who understood the working class, no matter their race, and his influence in the West End grew. By 1879, it was strong enough to land him a seat on Cincinnati's city council.

Many credited Cox with improving city life. Under his watch, Cincinnati modernized its police and fire departments, cleaned up its streets, regulated gambling and prostitution, and overhauled its water and sewer systems. He created a sense of order where there had been none, an emotional connection between the people and their government that hadn't existed before. Yet for all his so-called civic good, his reach did not come without consequence. He was also one of the key figures responsible for the failure of Cincinnati's subway system, a grand vision that never made it past the station.

But here's the question that lingers: Who in the Black community stood beside Cox, backed him, and helped solidify his rule?

At the time, Cincinnati had a number of prominent Black leaders, men who held sway in their communities, many of whom were deeply tied to the church. Faith and politics were intertwined, and Cox knew that. He also understood the power of the Black vote and made moves to increase participation, protecting working-class Black and immigrant neighborhoods just enough to keep his machine running.[15]

The question remains: Was it a partnership of opportunity, or was it manipulation disguised as progress?

It's possible—though highly unlikely—that Cox crossed paths with John Mercer Langston (1829–1897), Ohio's first Black attorney.[16] Their timelines just didn't quite align. By the time Cox was learning how to hustle through the backstreets of Cincinnati, Langston had already secured his law degree and was making a name for himself before eventually heading south to Virginia, where he'd go on to become the state's first Black member of Congress.

Now, Peter H. Clark (1829–1925)? That's a different story.

Clark was no ordinary figure—his name carried weight and not just because of his lineage. As the reputed (and controversial) son of explorer William Clark—a man who had enslaved Clark's Black mother before he eventually moved her and their biracial children to Cincinnati[17]—Peter H. Clark carved out his own legacy, distinct from the circumstances of his birth. It's likely that he and Cox's orbits overlapped, whether in passing or through shared political interests. The same could be said for George Washington Williams (1849–1891), a man of equal influence who, in 1876, took on the role of the pastor at Union Baptist Church, the city's oldest Black congregation,[18] planted firmly in the heart of the West End. By 1880, Williams had ascended to even greater heights, becoming the first Black elected official to the Ohio General Assembly, representing Hamilton County's Black community.[19]

But despite these rising figures and the sway of the Black vote, everything changed with the city election of 1921.

At the dawn of the twentieth century, Cincinnati's Black community had been pushing forward. The city was ahead of its time in school desegregation, at least compared to the rest of the country. By 1910, only one segregated high school remained: the Elm Street School in Walnut Hills, now known as Frederick Douglass Elementary. Progress? Sure. But when you zoom in, things weren't nearly as impressive as they might have seemed on the surface.

A few years later, the entire Cincinnati Public School System employed just seven Black teachers for fewer than three hundred Black students.[20] Seven. For the whole city. Now, that might not sound like much today (because it wasn't), but back in the early 1900s, it was still something. A foothold. Proof that the Black community wasn't waiting for change; they were making it happen themselves.

And if they were making strides in education, politics wasn't far behind.

For decades, Cox and his Republican machine had relied on the Black vote to push their candidates across the finish line. The promise was always the same: loyalty would be rewarded. But by the time 1921 rolled around, those promises were ringing hollow. Where were the Black leaders appointed to meaningful positions in city hall? Nowhere. How many Black leaders had secured seats in Hamilton County's power circles? None. The courthouse? The fire department? The answer was the same.[21] Time and again, the Black community had shown up for the Republican Party, but the party had failed to show up for them.

So, in 1921, they did something different.

Despite decades of Republican dominance—despite the shadow of Cox still looming over Cincinnati, even five years after his death—the Black community withdrew their support. And while the Republican Party still managed to clinch a victory, it didn't come with the help of Cincinnati's Black voters. Instead, that election year saw an entire Democratic slate and the full Farmer-Labor slate pull in votes, marking a turning point in the city's political landscape.

Cox's machine had held Cincinnati in its grip for forty years, but the tides were shifting. His reign had left its mark, but in the end, the very people he once counted on had begun to look elsewhere for the progress they had long been promised.

5

Covington's Eastside Neighborhood and Its Black Community

If Black communities had obituaries, the first paragraph of the historically Black Eastside neighborhood's might go something like this:

> *Covington's Eastside neighborhood, one of the region's most iconic Black communities, whose fostering of racial equality inspired generations, died today. Born in a time where Northern Kentucky's Black residents needed a place to live, work, and play where they were not degraded, the Eastside neighborhood dedicated its life to fighting for civil rights and social justice for its residents.*

When you've spent most of your entire life in one place, you start to learn its rhythms, its shortcuts, its secrets, the stories it holds in the cracks of its sidewalks and the corners of its old buildings. Covington, Kentucky, has always been that place for me. I made it my business to know this city beyond the obvious, beyond the expected. Not just the main roads but also the hidden cut-throughs, the forgotten paths, the unspoken routes that shaped my movement through the world. I guess you could say I was showing off a little, testing the limits of my own familiarity, seeing Covington from angles most people overlooked. But it wasn't just about navigating the city; it was about knowing it, really knowing it, in a way that made it feel like an extension of myself. And that knowing began in the city's Eastside neighborhood, a place deeply rooted in my family's history and in the broader story of Black resilience in greater Cincinnati and Northern Kentucky.

The Eastside, nestled in the northeastern stretch of Covington, is more than just a neighborhood, it's a testament, a statement of survival and perseverance. For generations, this community stood as a safe haven for Black families who were carving out their place in a world that often tried to push them aside. My grandfather Sherman Simpson was born in the 1930s right at the corner of Eighth and Greenup Streets, the heart of what was then a thriving Black neighborhood. His mother, Helen, raised him and his myriad brothers and sisters in a place where Black children played on stoops lined with neighbors who felt like extended family, where Black-owned businesses provided not just goods and services but also a sense of self-sufficiency, of ownership. The streets of Eastside weren't just roads—they were lifelines.

The neighborhood's roots stretch back to the late nineteenth century, when Black families, many fleeing the grip of segregation, settled here in search of something better. Bordered by the Licking River to the east and Madison Avenue to the west, Eastside quickly grew into a hub of Black life, a place where resilience wasn't just an idea, it was a necessity. In the face of exclusion from white establishments, Black entrepreneurs built their own. They created churches that became more than places of worship; they were community centers, political gathering spaces, sanctuaries in every sense of the word. Schools, barbershops, social halls, all were symbols of a community refusing to be erased.

Through the decades, Eastside bore witness to the defining moments of Black history—from the struggles of segregation to the victories of the civil rights movement. It was a place where young Black children learned their worth, where elders passed down wisdom on porches bathed in the golden glow of streetlights. But time and the forces of systemic displacement have reshaped the neighborhood. The neighborhood's once-dominant Black population has dwindled, gentrification creeping in like a slow tide, washing away families who had called Eastside home for generations. Some left by choice, but many were forced out by rising costs and shifting city priorities.

Patricia Fann, founder and editor of Covington's Suspension Press. *Kenton County Public Library*.

Yet the spirit of Black Eastside has never truly faded. Walk through the neighborhood today, and you'll still see remnants of what once was, a past that refuses to be forgotten. The buildings,

though weathered by time, stand tall. There's a weight in the air, a feeling that if you listen closely enough, you might still hear the echoes of children laughing in the alleys, jazz and gospel spilling out of open windows on warm summer nights.

And while the Black presence in Covington's Eastside neighborhood has diminished, its legacy remains intact. Former residents stay connected, showing up for each other in ways that transcend physical boundaries. Annual celebrations, community reunions, and storytelling sessions keep the history alive, ensuring that Eastside's story isn't lost to time or redevelopment. One of those events is the annual Old Timers Reunion Weekend, and it has been celebrated strong every year since the mid 1980s. Back then, the late David Housley and a group of graduates of the historic Lincoln Grant School in Covington, established the annual event to celebrate the history of the formerly segregated school and to keep alive the sense of place that many of the area's Black community shares. The bonds forged here were never just about geography; they were about something much deeper, something that distance and displacement could never undo.

Covington's Black residents and business owners have always been an integral part of the city's economic fabric. Their presence is stitched into its architecture, its art, its history. You can see it in the murals that dot the cityscape and pay tribute to Black excellence in the businesses that, despite

Opposite: A basketball tournament held annually during Old Timers Celebration in Randolph Park. *K.A. Simpson Collection.*

This page, top: Old Timers Celebration sign. *K.A. Simpson Collection.*

This page, bottom: Remembering the late David Housely, longtime organizer of Old Timers Celebration. *K.A. Simpson Collection.*

the odds, have persisted. And when the world slowed down during the COVID lockdown, I saw an opportunity to make sure those stories weren't just remembered but also shared. I created a self-guided walking tour that highlights the contributions of Black Covington—its landmarks, its people, the spaces that often go unnoticed but are vital to understanding the city's full history. That tour lives on today, available for free on the NKY Art Tours website, ready for anyone willing to take a walk through time.

And if you ever find yourself in Covington, reach out. If I'm around, I'll personally take you on the tour. Because some histories are best experienced firsthand in the places where the past still lingers, waiting to be heard. But until you do visit, read on to pick up more of what I am trying to throw down.

Covington's Black Business District

Historically, Black business districts have been lifelines, hubs of innovation, and symbols of self-sufficiency. Across the United States, these districts thrived, born out of necessity when segregation and racial discrimination blocked Black entrepreneurs from participating in mainstream economies. They were places where Black excellence was cultivated and allowed to flourish. And Covington's Eastside neighborhood was no exception.

Like so many others, Covington's Black business district stood as a testament to resilience. From the early 1900s through the 1960s, it was the beating heart of Black commerce in Northern Kentucky. Barbershops buzzed with conversation, beauty salons set the standard for style, and doctor's offices provided care in a world that often refused to acknowledge Black patients. Black dentists, attorneys, and shopkeepers set up along these blocks, creating a self-sustaining ecosystem where the community could invest in itself. These businesses weren't just places of transaction; they were places of gathering, connection, and pride.

I've always been fascinated by these districts, not just for their historical significance but also for the way they were systematically dismantled under the guise of "progress." It's a pattern we've seen play out across the country: prosperous Black communities wiped out, often through government-sanctioned policies like urban renewal, redlining, and highway expansion. Perhaps the most infamous example is the Greenwood District of Tulsa, Oklahoma, better known as Black Wall Street. A beacon of Black wealth and self-determination, it was obliterated in the 1921 Tulsa Race Massacre, an act of racial terror that left an entire community in ruins.

But Tulsa wasn't alone. Bronzeville in Chicago. Sweet Auburn in Atlanta. Harlem in New York City. These districts weren't just economic hubs; they were cultural powerhouses, shaping the music, literature, and social movements that defined Black America. They provided a roadmap for what Black economic freedom could look like—a roadmap that was repeatedly erased, often violently, but never forgotten.

Covington's Black business district may not be as widely known as those in major cities, but its impact was just as significant for the people who relied on it. This was where Black entrepreneurs could build legacies, where Black professionals could practice their crafts, where Black families could shop without facing hostility. It was a space carved out in a world that had tried to shut them out.

And just as Black business districts cultivated economic independence, they also nurtured intellectual and social leadership. Take James McCune Smith, the first Black student to earn a medical degree. Denied entry into American medical schools because of his race, Smith pursued his education at the University of Glasgow in Scotland, earning his degree in 1837. A prolific writer and abolitionist, Smith used his platform to dismantle racist pseudoscience and champion the inevitable rise of Black excellence.[22] Frederick Douglass once said of him, "No man in this country more thoroughly understands the whole struggle between freedom and slavery than does Dr. Smith, and his heart is as broad as his understanding." Smith made contributions not only in medicine but also in the larger fight for justice, proving that Black intellect and leadership were unstoppable forces, despite every effort to suppress them.

And Northern Kentucky had its very own Dr. Smith.

He walked the streets of Covington, practiced in the community, and left a legacy that deserves to be remembered. His story, like so many others, is woven into the history of Covington's Black business district, a history that still lingers in the foundations of buildings, in the echoes of stories passed down, in the lessons of resilience that continue to shape the present.

Because while these districts may have been physically dismantled, their spirit endures. And their impact? That can never be erased.

DR. JAMES RANDOLPH

Dr. James Randolph was Black physician and the first to be on the staff of Covington's St. Elizabeth Hospital. Most of the Black children born in Covington between 1922 and 1958 were delivered by Dr. Randolph. His historic marker is included in the aforementioned tour. But folks in Northern Kentucky didn't stop there. We named a park after him, too.

I came to appreciate Dr. Randolph's supernova-like talent very early in life. I heard stories about the times he would come and look after not only my great-grandmother but also my grandmother and mother when they were growing up. And there was this park named after him just a few blocks away from my house that had an amazing swimming pool. That was the lifeline of my summer life growing up.

RANDOLPH PARK

There are several parks named after notable Black doctors throughout the country, but one example is the Dr. Charles Drew Park in Arlington, Virginia. Dr. Charles Drew was a pioneering Black physician, researcher, and surgeon known for his work in blood transfusions. He was a key figure in developing techniques for the long-term preservation of blood plasma, which was crucial during World War II and laid the foundation for modern blood banks.

Dr. Charles Drew Park in Arlington is a tribute to his legacy and contributions to medicine. It serves as a reminder of the importance of his work and the impact he had on healthcare and society.

The park in Covington named after Dr. James Randolph has served as a safe space for Eastside residents to gather. Since 1986, the park has hosted the annual Old Timers Festival, when community members come back from across the country to celebrate the rich culture of the Eastside neighborhood. Randolph Park has a swimming pool, basketball courts, a playground, and a picnic shelter with a grill.

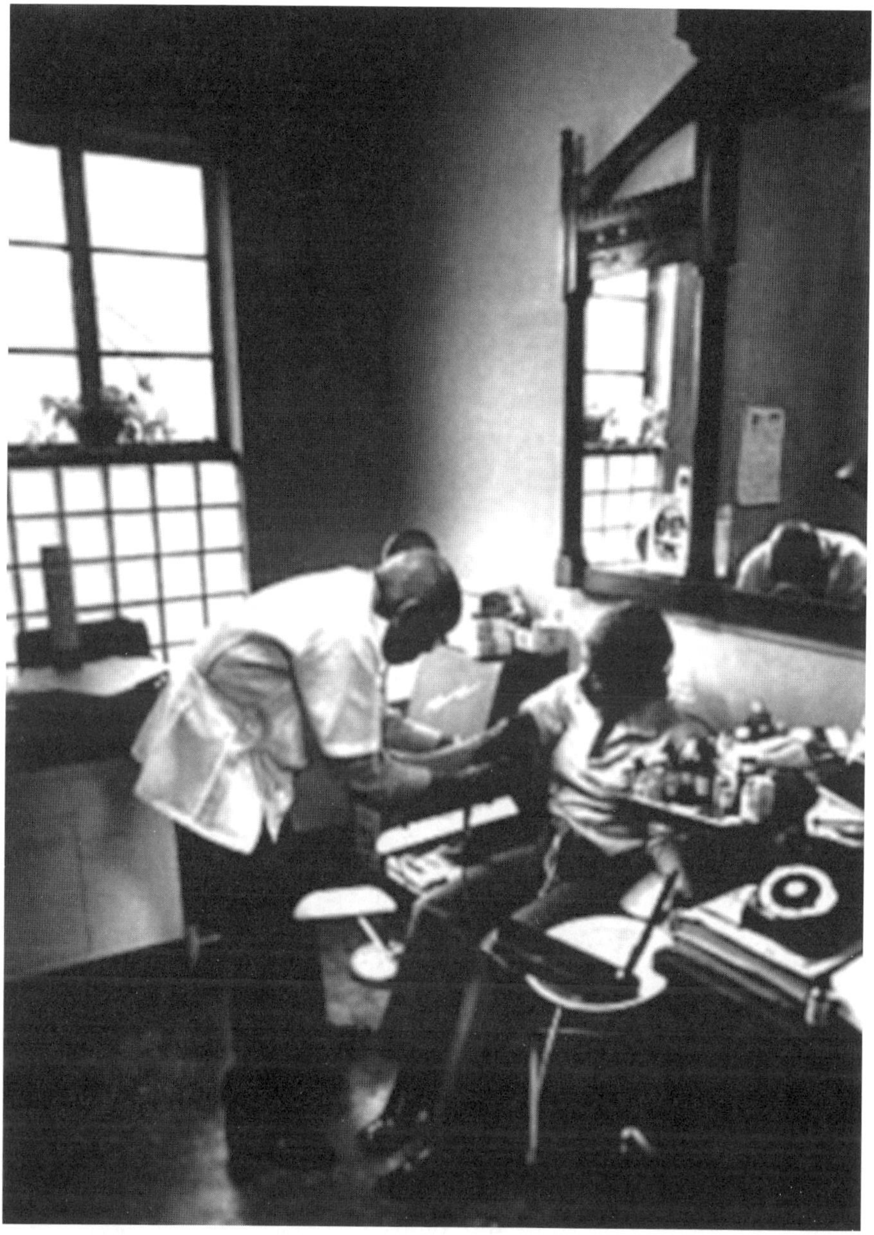

Opposite: James E. Randolph, MD. *Kenton County Public Library*.

Above: James Randolph, MD, practicing medicine. *Kenton County Public Library*.

It was the park where the Black community gathered in Covington. I have fond memories of being relegated to the space, nestled directly within the Eastside neighborhood, many times throughout the year when the weather was nice. In addition, it was one of the only places where the Black community felt comfortable at the swimming pool. Yes, there were swimming pools throughout Covington, Kentucky, but at least for me, the swimming pool at Randolph Park is where I saw people who looked like me. One of my fondest memories is being six years old and swimming there, my mom trying to drag me from the pool. But Boy George smashing out a song that I was vibing to, and I didn't want to leave. I remember pitching a fit until my mother dragged me from that pool. Needless to say, I didn't get to hear the end of the song.

Covington's Black Church Institutions

Until around the early 1990s, I was a good little ol' church boy. I went to church with my mom most Sundays. I grew up in a Catholic school, and I even sang in the choir. Actually, one of my fondest memories from my childhood is getting baptized at Our Savior Church, a historically Black Catholic church in Covington's Eastside neighborhood. But in the 1990s, I was a rebellious teenager, and I began to read the "Good Book." I came across a passage that characterized Jesus as something other than what I had been told he was. It says in Revelation 1:14–15 that Jesus's skin was a darker hue and that his hair was wooly in texture. The hairs of his head, it says, "were white as white wool, white as snow. His eyes were like a flame of fire, his feet were like burnished bronze, refined as in a furnace."[23]

But all the pictures of Jesus I'd ever been shown depicted him with blond hair and blue eyes. The only thing I could think was that Jesus was a Black man—and the church had been lying to me.

Despite my own idyllic woes, Black churches have historically been central institutions in many Black neighborhoods, serving as not only places of worship but also community centers, gathering spaces, and hubs for social activism. These churches have played a crucial role in fostering solidarity, providing support, and promoting cultural identity within Black communities.

In predominantly Black neighborhoods across the United States, you can often find churches that cater specifically to the Black community.

These churches may vary in denomination, size, and architectural style, but they share a common purpose of serving the spiritual and social needs of their congregations.

These churches often host various community events, social programs, and outreach initiatives aimed at addressing the unique challenges facing Black neighborhoods, such as poverty, inequality, and systemic racism. They also serve as platforms for promoting social justice, civil rights, and empowerment within the community.

Examples of historically significant Black churches in predominantly Black neighborhoods include Abyssinian Baptist Church in Harlem, New York; Ebenezer Baptist Church in Atlanta, Georgia; and Greater Bethel AME Church in Chicago, Illinois. These churches have been important landmarks in their respective communities and continue to play vital roles in shaping the social, cultural, and spiritual fabric of Black neighborhoods.

Ninth Street Missionary Baptist Church

Since 1869, the congregation had been coming together, first in modest spaces and then in a place they could truly call their own. But it wasn't until around 1900 that they found a permanent home on Ninth Street, a location that would become a cornerstone of faith and resilience for generations to come.

In 1914, with hope in their hearts and a vision for the future, the congregation laid the first cornerstone for the church that still stands today. But progress came slowly. Brick by brick, year by year, the building took shape, a testament to the patience and dedication of the community. It wasn't until 1921 that its construction was finally complete, marking a new chapter for the church and the people who had built it—not just with materials but also with unwavering faith.

But their faith would be tested again. In 1937, a great flood of the Ohio River came, its waters rising far beyond Ninth Street, swallowing homes, businesses, and history itself. The church was not spared. The basement, once a place of safekeeping, became a vault of destruction. Decades of records—births, baptisms, marriages, the very documentation of a people's existence—were lost beneath the floodwaters. The stories remained, passed down through voices and memories, but the tangible proof of their journey had been washed away.

Even in disaster, the congregation refused to be displaced. Until the church could be restored, they found sanctuary in the auditorium of Lincoln Grant School, another pillar of the community, another space where Black resilience had long been nurtured. And when the church reopened, it stood not just as a building but also as a survivor.

This was never just about brick and mortar. It was about the people who kept coming back, who rebuilt, who refused to let disaster—natural or man-made—erase what they had created. The church, like the community it served, endured. And that endurance is its true foundation.

FIRST BAPTIST CHURCH

In 1864, a small but determined group of twenty-two believers came together to form what would become a cornerstone of faith in the community. Their church was more than just a place of worship; it was a refuge, a gathering place, and a symbol of perseverance in a world that often sought to push them to the margins.

But as with many things built from passion and conviction, division found its way in. Not long after its founding, the congregation split. For a time, they reunited, attempting to mend the fractures that had formed, but some within the group felt called to carve their own path. That division gave rise to what would become Ninth Street Baptist Church, another beacon of faith and resilience that still stands today.

Adversity, however, was never far from their story. In 1915, a tornado tore through their community, leaving destruction in its wake and reducing their place of worship to rubble. But faith isn't held within walls; it is carried in the hearts of those who refuse to let destruction have the final word. Determined to rebuild, the congregation found a new home, one that still stands today, a testament to their endurance, their unity, and their belief in something greater than themselves.

Their legacy is quite literally written into the landscape of the city. The church is immortalized on the Jacob Price riverfront mural, a visual reminder of the strength and perseverance that has defined this congregation for generations. It stands not just as a building, but also as a story, one of struggle, resilience, and an unshakable commitment to faith.

Our Savior Catholic Church

Tucked within the heart of Covington's Eastside neighborhood, Our Savior Catholic Church stands as a living testament to faith, resilience, and the enduring legacy of Black Catholicism in Northern Kentucky. For generations, it has been more than a house of worship; it has been a refuge, a community center, and a symbol of perseverance in the face of adversity.

The church was founded in the mid-1900s during an era of segregation, Our Savior was born out of necessity as a place where Black Catholics could gather, worship freely, and find spiritual guidance without the shadow of discrimination. It was a church built not just with bricks and mortar but also with the unwavering determination of those who refused to be excluded from their faith. The challenges were many—financial struggles, social barriers, and the constant pushback of a world that often sought to deny the Black community space—but the parishioners held firm. Their faith was their foundation, and from it, they built something lasting.

Our Savior has never been just a church; it has been a cultural and spiritual anchor, shaping the lives of its members through worship, education, and community outreach. Gospel choirs filled the sanctuary with soul-stirring music. Events and programs celebrated the rich heritage of Black Catholics. It was a place where generations came together, where history was honored, and where young people found role models in the elders who had carried the torch before them.

Its origins are deeply rooted in a pivotal moment. In the summer of 1943, Bishop Howard of the Diocese of Covington laid the foundation for a new church and school on East Tenth Street, designed specifically to serve the Black Catholic community in Northern Kentucky. The school may no longer stand, but the church remains, an enduring beacon of faith and the last Black Catholic parish in the Diocese of Covington.

I know this story intimately because I lived it. I was a member of this church, part of the dwindling but proud class of Black Catholics in Northern Kentucky. And recently, I had the rare opportunity to flip through the baptismal records of Our Savior—all handwritten, all preserved in a single book dating back to the mid-1900s. It was like turning the pages of time itself. I recognized names, people a generation older than me, people I had grown up admiring. Then came the names of my peers. And then, there it was—my own baptismal record. I won't lie, I might have shed a tear or two.

Today, Our Savior continues its mission, standing strong as a vibrant, welcoming space for all who seek spiritual nourishment and community.

As the last Black Catholic church in the diocese, it carries the weight of history on its shoulders, a symbol of resilience, faith, and the unshakable power of community.

Reflecting on its history, I am reminded of the strength and determination of those who came before us, the founders, the parishioners, the leaders who refused to let this church fade. Their legacy is a call to action, urging us to support and uplift this historic institution so that its story, its faith, and its impact live on for generations to come.

Jacob Price, His Home, and His Legacy

Beginning in the early 2000s, Covington's Eastside neighborhood found itself at the center of an all too familiar story, one in which the march of gentrification tramples over history, displacing longtime Black residents, erasing cultural landmarks, and widening the economic divide. Nowhere is this more evident than in the transformation of the Jacob Price Housing Projects, a once-thriving community that bore the name of one of Covington's most influential Black pioneers.

Gentrification is often painted as progress—a shiny new coat of urban renewal—but for those on the losing end of the equation, it's nothing short of a slow-motion upheaval. The process follows a predictable script: wealthier residents move in, property values and rents skyrocket, and the people who built these neighborhoods, who have called them home for generations, are forced out. It's not just about losing homes. It's about losing the very fabric of a community, a sense of belonging, and the cultural legacy that made these neighborhoods what they were in the first place.

In Covington, the ill effects of passive gentrification have been particularly stark. The Jacob Price Homes, built in 1939 as an affordable housing development,[24] once stood as a testament to the resilience and strength of the Black community. But as the city's priorities shifted and developers saw an opportunity, these homes were deemed expendable. Residents were promised they could return once the new housing was built. That promise, like so many before it, was hollow. Today, in place of the Jacob Price Homes, stands a mixed-income, market-rate housing development where only a handful of former residents have been able to return.

It's a story that plays out time and time again across America, where the ghosts of once-thriving Black communities whisper beneath sleek new condos and craft coffee shops. Imagine, if you will, a surreal sitcom: hipster cafés appear overnight, yoga studios dot the corners where barbershops and soul food restaurants once stood, and longtime residents find themselves watching a world they no longer recognize unfold around them. One day, it's *Good Times*. The next, it's *Friends*. The difference? The original cast never got a fair chance to stay.

The loss of the Jacob Price Homes is not just a story of displacement; it's cultural erasure. Before the demolition, this neighborhood was a tight-knit community where families lived for generations. Children played in the courtyards, neighbors looked out for each other, and a shared history bound people together. But when the bulldozers came, they didn't just tear down buildings; they tore apart a community's sense of identity.

And this isn't just about buildings and businesses; it's about a man, a legacy, a name that meant something to the people who lived here. Jacob Price wasn't just a name on a housing project. He was a leader, a minister, an entrepreneur, and an advocate for Black education in Covington. Born a free man of color, Price moved to Covington at the age of twenty, and by twenty-four, he had become the pastor of the area's Black Baptist church. Under his leadership, the church flourished and later split to form the First Baptist Church and Ninth Street Baptist Church, both of which still hold their place in Covington's history.

Beyond the pulpit, Price was a staunch advocate for Black education. He helped establish a school for Black Americans, paving the way for William Grant School, the first Black high school in Covington. His own daughter, Anna, was among the school's first graduates and went on to teach at the school. And then there was his business acumen—his lumber business, started in 1881, became a major success, employing Black workers and providing materials for countless buildings in the area. That lumberyard, once located at 426 and 428 Madison Avenue, is long gone, now just another parking lot for nearby businesses.

But Price's impact cannot be erased so easily. His name lives on, enshrined in a Kentucky Historical Marker at the corner of Ninth and Greenup Streets, a silent reminder of the contributions he made to this city. His face, immortalized in the Covington Floodwall Mural Series, watches over a landscape that has changed in ways he might never have imagined. The bottom right corner of that mural depicts the government-funded housing project that once carried his name, a project that no longer stands.

The displacement of the Black community in Covington is not just about real estate; it's about systemic inequities that make it difficult for Black families to stay rooted. The rising property taxes, the lack of affordable housing options, and the economic pressures that come with gentrification create a perfect storm that forces people out, whether they want to leave or not. Many former Jacob Price residents found themselves scattered across the region, disconnected from the community that had once been their home.

When the Jacob Price Homes were demolished, city officials framed it as progress. They promised new housing, new opportunities, a better future. But progress for whom? For the Black families who were uprooted, the promises never completely materialized. The number of affordable housing units in the redevelopment fell far short of what was needed and promised, and strict application processes ensured that many original residents couldn't return. What stands in place of Jacob Price now is a development that caters to a different demographic, one with more disposable income and less connection to the neighborhood's history.

In Covington, the Eastside neighborhood was a community rich with Black history, resilience, and a deep-rooted sense of identity. The loss of the Jacob Price Homes is a loss for everyone who believes in the importance of preserving Black history, honoring the legacies of those who came before us, and ensuring that progress doesn't come at the expense of erasure.

But history is not so easily washed away. The memory of Jacob Price—of the people who lived in the homes that bore his name, of the culture that thrived here—remains woven into the foundation of this city. The question is: Who will fight to keep this history alive? Who will stand up and demand that the progress of a city not erase a people? Because if we don't, the only thing left of Jacob Price will be his mural and a footnote in history. And that is not enough.

OTHER NOTABLE INSTITUTIONS AND BUILDINGS

Henry Wenzel Building

Nestled in the heart of Covington, Kentucky, the Henry Wenzel building stands as a quiet yet significant testament to the city's layered history. Built in the late nineteenth century, this unassuming structure once served as more than just a brick-and-mortar front; it was a lifeline for Black musicians traveling through the segregated South and Midwest.

During the Jim Crow era, Black performers—many of them legends in jazz, the blues, and soul—faced rampant discrimination while on tour. Hotels, restaurants, and venues across the country often refused them service, forcing them to seek alternative accommodations wherever they could find them. The Henry Wenzel building became one of those rare spaces where these artists could find shelter, a warm meal, and a sense of community.

Though not technically located in Covington's Eastside neighborhood, this building, for a short time, was one of the few places where Black travelers could stay without fear of harassment or expulsion. The Wenzel building, like many structures across the country, held a boardinghouse that welcomed Black musicians who otherwise had nowhere else to turn. It wasn't just a place to sleep; it was a refuge, a stop on the long road between cities, and sometimes even a venue for impromptu jam sessions that would never make it into the history books but lived on in the hearts of those who witnessed them.

Boardinghouses like the one inside the Henry Wenzel building operated out of necessity. They provided not only a bed but also a communal space where Black musicians could gather, share stories, and connect with the local Black community. Some musicians would arrive after performing at whites-only clubs, where they entertained segregated crowds but couldn't sit at the bar afterward or use the front entrance. Here at the Wenzel building, they found a different world, one where they were embraced, respected, and understood.

The accommodations in buildings like these were often modest—a simple room with a bed, a chair, and perhaps a small writing desk was the standard. Yet these spaces carried immeasurable value. They were safe havens in a world that sought to keep Black artists on the fringes. While some musicians stayed in well-known Black-owned hotels or in boardinghouses listed in publications like *The Negro Motorist Green Book*, others found temporary residence in establishments like the Henry Wenzel building, places not widely recorded but essential in the fabric of Black musical history.

The cultural impact of buildings like this cannot be overstated. They played a crucial role in sustaining the music and the movement, allowing artists to continue their work despite the systemic racism that sought to suppress them. The walls of the Wenzel building, if they could speak, would echo with the stories of those who passed through, stories of resilience, artistry, and perseverance in the face of adversity.

Today, as Covington undergoes waves of redevelopment and gentrification, structures like the Henry Wenzel building stand as reminders of a past that should not be forgotten. Though the boardinghouse is long gone and its rooms no longer serve as rest stops for weary musicians, its legacy endures in the echoes of the past. The building remains a physical testament to the resilience of Black artists and the communities that supported them, an emblem of an era when music was both a form of expression and a means of survival.

The Henry Wenzel building is more than just a structure; it is a symbol of the ingenuity and perseverance of Black musicians who, against all odds, found ways to navigate a world that often tried to keep them silent. It is a piece of Covington's history that speaks to the broader Black experience, a reminder that even in the darkest times, there were always places of refuge, where music played on and the spirit remained unbroken.

Overall, Black musicians faced significant challenges in finding safe and comfortable accommodations during the era of segregation.

Although its address is on Madison Avenue, this building is actually located behind the Chops, Cheese & Chives store and can be accessed via Tobacco Alley, just to the north of the store. In its 150 years, the building has been used for many purposes, but it most significantly housed the Black Odd Fellows Hall on its third floor. The Odd Fellows is a social organization whose historic purpose is to "visit the sick, relieve the distressed, bury the dead and educate the orphan." Today, it is a very diverse international organization whose members take active roles in helping improve their communities.

The building, often called the Pickle Factory (because, at one time, it was used for this purpose) has been renovated for a first-floor commercial tenant and eight short-term rental units on the upper floors.

Kenton County Public Library and the Black Community

The roots of the Kenton County Public Library can be traced back to 1899, when several distinguished citizens of Covington, Kentucky, convened to discuss the need for a public library for the area's citizens.

The Covington branch of the Kenton County Public Library in Kentucky was was never officially segregated, although the practice of segregation was common in the region during the Jim Crow era. The library's commitment to inclusivity and equal access to all members of the community made it a beacon of progressiveness in the area.

The Carnegie Arts Center

Some buildings whisper history through their brick and mortar. Others stand as bold testaments to the ideals they were built on. The Carnegie in Covington, Kentucky, is the latter—a place where past and present converge, where knowledge once reigned and creativity now flourishes.

Originally constructed as a public library, the Carnegie was more than just a grand Beaux-Arts structure; it was a symbol of access, of intellectual freedom. At a time when segregation was the rule rather than the exception, the Carnegie stood apart, one of the few libraries in the country to never bar entry based on race. While countless other institutions upheld the boundaries of Jim Crow laws, this space remained open, a quiet but powerful act of defiance against the tide of exclusion.

But time transforms even the most steadfast of spaces. Today, the Carnegie has evolved into something even greater: a thriving arts center, where stories continue to be told, not through books alone but also through performance, canvas, and the raw expression of human creativity. The echo of turned pages has given way to the hum of rehearsals in its theater, the quiet contemplation of art in its galleries, and the spark of inspiration ignited in its classrooms.

La Salette Garden Apartments

Some buildings hold memories in their walls, echoes of laughter in hallways, the hurried footsteps of students late to class, the quiet resolve of young minds shaped by lessons far beyond textbooks. The La Salette Garden Apartments may now stand as modern housing, but the foundation was laid in the name of education, progress, and the quiet revolution of desegregation in Northern Kentucky.

Before it became a residence, this structure was home to La Salette Academy, an all-girls Catholic high school that, in its time, was one of the first institutions in the region to desegregate and welcome Black students. At a time when racial barriers loomed large over the American South and Midwest, La Salette was an outlier, a school that chose inclusion over exclusion, progress over prejudice.

Imagine it: young Black girls walking through these doors, some for the first time, stepping into an educational space once deemed off-limits. Their presence was more than symbolic; it was transformative. Within these walls, friendships formed across the artificial boundaries of race, education flourished in an environment of quiet resistance, and a new generation of thinkers and leaders found their footing.

Today, the building wears a different identity as La Salette Garden Apartments. The classrooms have been repurposed into homes, but the spirit of change remains. Those walls, once filled with chalkboards and desks, now house families, yet the legacy of its past lingers, a reminder that progress, once set in motion, never truly fades. It has evolved from a groundbreaking institution of learning to a residence that still shelters stories—of struggle, of triumph, and of the ongoing fight to make inclusion not the exception but the rule.

Governor's Pointe Condos

Before luxury condos and modern living, before the quiet hum of a transformed space, the main building of what is now Governor's Pointe Condos stood as something far more urgently needed—a place where life entered the world, where the sick found refuge, and where, against the tides of segregation, doors opened for those who were often left in the cold.

Built in 1914, Booth Memorial Hospital was not just another medical facility in Northern Kentucky; it was a quiet rebellion against the racial barriers that shaped healthcare in the early twentieth century. In a time when hospitals across the region denied or severely restricted care for Black patients, Booth Memorial stood apart. Here, the oath to heal extended beyond racial lines, offering Black patients access to medical attention that, elsewhere, was often delayed or denied.

Imagine what that meant. For many Black families, Booth wasn't just a hospital—it was a lifeline. The sight of a Black mother stepping through its doors, knowing she could give birth in a facility that wouldn't turn her away. A father, injured on the job, receiving treatment without being sent to the back door or the basement. A child, feverish and frail, tended to by hands that saw only a patient, not a problem.

Over time, as medicine advanced and segregation's grip loosened, Booth Memorial evolved, eventually closing its doors as a hospital and transforming into the Governor's Pointe Condominiums. The surgical suites and maternity wards gave way to high-end residences. Its hallways, once filled with nurses and patients, are now lined with modern décor and quiet domesticity.

But make no mistake—history lingers here. The walls that once heard the cries of newborns and the relief of families now stand as silent witnesses to an era of change. Booth Memorial was more than a hospital; it was a statement that care should not be a privilege of race but a right of humanity.

We are never going to regain this thriving community. We're never again going to see the time when we were able to congregate in our own neighborhood in a place where we felt safe. I'm not necessarily saying that we should even try to bring these things back, but we have to remember how great they once were and continue to celebrate the people of the past and their influence on the people of the future.

6

CINCINNATI'S CONNECTION TO *UNCLE TOM'S CABIN*

Some memories cling to you like ink on a page, etched deep, refusing to fade. You remember where you were, what you were doing, and sometimes even the way the air smelled or how the sun cast its light when certain moments unfolded. One of my earliest memories is wrapped in the warmth of a visit to my great-aunt's home.

Aunt Sara lived perched on a hill in downtown Cincinnati, where the world stretched wide before my young eyes. From her vantage point, you could see across the river to Covington, Kentucky, the place I called home. I wasn't much older than a toddler the first time I stood at her window, looking down at the movement of life below—the hum of cars, the shuffle of people, the way the city seemed to breathe. It was the first time I witnessed so much at once, and it fascinated me.

The trip from my home in Northern Kentucky to Aunt Sara's house in Cincinnati's Evanston neighborhood took only fifteen minutes, but to me, it felt like crossing into another world. These visits happened every few weeks, and each time, they filled my young mind with wonder. They meant something more than just a family gathering—they were adventures. The winding roads, the city's towering buildings, the bridges that stretched over the Ohio River—it was all so grand, so full of possibility.

But there was one sight on that drive that, for years, I overlooked.

On Gilbert Avenue, near what is now Martin Luther King Jr. Boulevard, stood a home, stoic, unwavering, tucked into the city's landscape. I passed by it countless times without giving it a second thought. To a child, it was

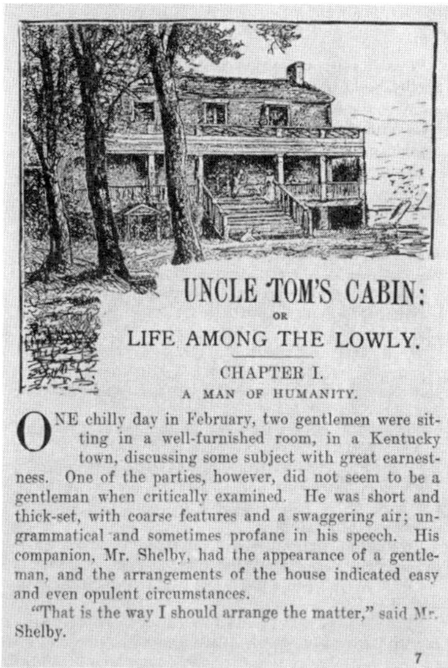

UNCLE TOM'S CABIN:

OR

LIFE AMONG THE LOWLY.

CHAPTER I.

A MAN OF HUMANITY.

ONE chilly day in February, two gentlemen were sitting in a well-furnished room, in a Kentucky town, discussing some subject with great earnestness. One of the parties, however, did not seem to be a gentleman when critically examined. He was short and thick-set, with coarse features and a swaggering air; ungrammatical and sometimes profane in his speech. His companion, Mr. Shelby, had the appearance of a gentleman, and the arrangements of the house indicated easy and even opulent circumstances.

"That is the way I should arrange the matter," said Mr. Shelby.

7

Uncle Tom's Cabin. Library of Congress.

just another old house. Nothing about it called to me then. But as I grew older, I came to understand that history doesn't always announce itself in grand gestures. Sometimes, it stands quietly, waiting for you to notice.

That house—the one I had glanced at so many times in passing—held the story of one of Cincinnati's most influential families. It was the home of Lyman Beecher, a towering figure in nineteenth-century America. A Congregationalist minister, theologian, and fierce reformer, Beecher was a leading advocate of the temperance movement and a passionate voice in the fight against slavery.[25] His influence shaped not only the city but also the nation.

But perhaps even more well-known than Lyman Beecher was his daughter, Harriet Beecher Stowe.

The very house I had unknowingly ignored was the Harriet Beecher Stowe House, a landmark of history, a place where ideas that would shake the foundation of a divided nation were once formed. Harriet lived there from 1832 to 1836, and during those years, she became deeply entrenched in the abolitionist movement. The city of Cincinnati, with its proximity to the slaveholding state of Kentucky, was a hotbed of tension and resistance. It was here that Harriet saw firsthand the horrors of slavery, experiences that would later shape *Uncle Tom's Cabin*, the novel that set fire to the conscience of a country.

That house was not just a relic of the past; it was a witness to history in motion. It stood as a space where ideas of justice, faith, and rebellion intertwined. It was where words were sharpened into weapons against oppression. And for all those years, I had unknowingly driven past it, never realizing I was moving through a landscape stitched with stories that had shaped the world.

Looking back, I think about that young version of myself, staring out at a city that seemed so alive, so full of movement. I think about the things we fail to notice until we're ready, the history that lingers around us, waiting for us to see it.

Now, when I pass that house on Gilbert Avenue, I see more than brick and mortar. I see the weight of history pressing against time, the echoes of a young woman who dared to write against injustice, and the lesson that some stories—no matter how quietly they stand—demand to be remembered.

***

Uncle Tom's Cabin, published in 1852, was a groundbreaking work that helped to fuel the abolitionist cause, and it is credited with galvanizing public opinion against slavery in the years leading up to the Civil War. The novel's impact was so profound that when President Abraham Lincoln met Stowe in 1862, he reportedly greeted her by saying, "So you're the little woman who wrote the book that started this great war."[26]

Barbara Furr, a former board member of the Friends of the Harriet Beecher Stowe House, said:

> *This home was built for Harriet's father and stepmother. He came here to Cincinnati to be the president of a theological seminary that stood about a quarter of a mile from here. This was the home built for the president of the college, and it was a very important place in Cincinnati at the time and still is today. The seminary was built as a place to train Presbyterian ministers. Harriet was one of the last children born to Lyman and his first wife, Roxanna Foote Beecher. Harriet Beecher first arrived in Cincinnati and worked as a teacher with her sister, Kathryn. Katryn came here to set up a school, and Harriet came along.*

Christina Hartleib, Harriet Beecher Stowe House's executive director, in an Ohio Connection YouTube video, said:

> *Harriet Beecher stow is really the epitome of voice. Harriet writes the most important anti-slavery novel ever and yet she's a white woman who grew up in New England. So, how is she able to accomplish this task? It's because of the eighteen years she lived here in Cincinnati. It's where she learned the things that she needed to learn, met the people she needed to meet in order to be able to write* Uncle Tom's Cabin. *In 1943, when a group of local citizens got together and said that they wanted to create a memorial to Harriet and an African American cultural center using the Beecher family home, they spearheaded the effort to raise money to turn it into a historic site. Their ultimate goal was to create a lighthouse of goodwill and understanding.*[27]

Today, the Harriet Beecher Stowe House stands as a tribute to Stowe's legacy and a reminder of the struggles and triumphs of the abolitionist movement. The house has been restored and is open to the public for tours, offering visitors a chance to learn more about Stowe's life and work and the history of the antislavery movement in America.

JAMES BRADLEY, LANE SEMINARY, AND THE ABOLITION DEBATES

Lane Seminary, under the formidable leadership of Lyman Beecher, was not just an institution of higher learning in Cincinnati—it was a battleground. In the 1830s, at a time when the country teetered on the edge of moral reckoning, Lane became a crucible for some of the most fervent voices in the abolitionist movement. Within its walls, young men wrestled with the defining question of their era: Could a nation built on the promise of liberty continue to justify the enslavement of human beings?

The defining moment of Lane's radical transformation came in 1834 with what would become known as the Lane Seminary Debates. These weren't just intellectual exercises; they were fiery, impassioned confrontations with the darkest truths of American society. Over eighteen evenings, for two and a half hours each night, students, faculty, and local community members engaged in intense deliberations on the morality, legality, and future of slavery. The debates, spearheaded by the renowned abolitionist Theodore Weld, didn't just challenge minds—they ignited a movement.

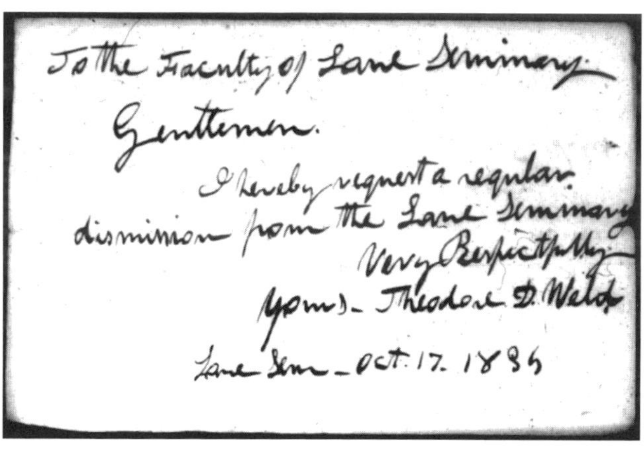
To the Faculty of Lane Seminary.
Gentlemen.
I hereby request a regular dismission from the Lane Seminary
Very Respectfully
Yours— Theodore D. Weld
Lane Sem—Oct. 17. 1835

Theodore Dwight Weld's letter of dismission, "THEODORE DWIGHT WELD 1835-10-17." *Harriet Beecher Stowe House.*

Lane Theological Seminary. *Walnut Hills Redevelopment Foundation.*

Seventeen students, many of them men who had encountered slavery firsthand, took the floor. Among them was James A. Thome, the son of a wealthy Kentucky slaveholder whose transformation from an heir to an advocate shook the room. There was also Huntington Lyman, a Connecticut native who had spent years in Louisiana,[28] his voice carrying the weight of lived experience. And then there was James Bradley, a man who, by all odds, wasn't supposed to be there at all.

Bradley's story defied convention. Born into slavery, he didn't just escape its grasp; he carved his own path to freedom armed with nothing but determination and an unshakable thirst for knowledge. His very presence at Lane was an act of rebellion. He was a living testament to the power of self-liberation. Long before I ever penned my first book, I had the honor of writing about Bradley for the first edition of the *Northern Kentucky Encyclopedia* back in the early 2000s:

> *James Bradley, a slave who became an abolitionist, was born into slavery in Africa and as an infant was taken to South Carolina. He was sold to a slave trader who then sold him to the owner of Bradley Plantation in Pendleton County, Kentucky, from which Bradley derived his surname. As a teenager, he moved to Arkansas with his owner, performing normal duties by day. By night, with the permission from his master, he did odd jobs for other plantation owners and received wages. On many days, Bradley was able to muster only a few hours of sleep. After five years, he had saved $700, which he used to purchase his freedom.*
>
> *Once free, he briefly returned to Northern Kentucky before entering into the free territory in Ohio, crossing the Ohio River at Covington. Soon afterward, Bradley was admitted to the Lane Theological Seminary in Cincinnati. As the first African American student there, he joined in the seminary's abolitionist movement, participating in the famous Lane Debates of 1834. He later attended the Sheffield Manual Labor Institute, a branch of Oberlin College in northern Ohio, for one year. From then on, Bradley appears to be lost to history.*
>
> *A statue of Bradley was placed along Riverside Drive in Covington, marking roughly where he crossed the Ohio River into Ohio. Created by sculptor George Danhires, the bronze statue has dimensions 49 in. by 29 in. by 53 in., with a base of 28 in. by 8 in. by 17 in. Bradley is depicted sitting on a park bench reading a book, a tribute to a man who, in difficult circumstances, taught himself to read.*[29]

Even then, his story struck me as more than just historic record. It was a lesson in the audacity of hope.

Bradley's journey wasn't just about breaking the rules; it was about rewriting them entirely. His existence challenged every argument that sought to justify slavery. He had been shackled by the system and still found a way to rise. And at Lane, his voice, once silenced by chains, was now leading the charge for change.

The Lane Seminary Debates didn't end quietly. The ideas sparked within those halls could not be contained. In response to the abolitionist fervor swelling among the students, Lane's trustees, fearful of the controversy, attempted to suppress the movement. But the students refused to back down. Many of them, including Weld and his followers, left the seminary in protest, taking their firebrand activism elsewhere, most notably to Oberlin College, which became a stronghold for abolitionist thought.

The ripples of what happened at Lane spread far beyond Cincinnati. The debates emboldened the national antislavery movement, further radicalized its leaders, and set the stage for the greater struggles to come. In a city where freedom and bondage existed in uneasy proximity, Lane Seminary had become more than a school; it was frontline in the fight for justice.

Even today, as I walk the streets of Cincinnati, I think of the voices that once echoed through those halls. I think of Bradley, Weld, and Thome, of the nights spent locked in debate, of the minds changed and the futures altered. I think of how history doesn't just happen; it is forged in moments of defiance, shaped by those willing to stand, speak, and refuse to yield.

The Lane Seminary Debates were a seismic shift in the minds of those who dared to challenge the status quo. These debates didn't just end when the students left the room; they sparked a transformation that rippled far beyond Cincinnati. For men like Theodore Weld, this was a defining moment, a trial by fire that forged some of the most relentless abolitionists of their time. They weren't just discussing change; they were stepping into the arena and becoming the change.

But the impact of these debates went beyond individual awakenings. They raised a question that remains just as urgent today: What role does education play in shaping social progress? The very foundation of Lane Seminary trembled under the weight of these discussions, and the aftershocks could be felt far beyond the seminary walls. Suddenly, education wasn't just about theology or philosophy; it was about justice. It was about using knowledge as a weapon against oppression.

And here's the thing—this wasn't just a moment locked in history books. The legacy of the Lane Seminary Debates is still alive, a testament to what happens when people gather, challenge each other, and push society toward something greater. It's proof that ideas have power. That classrooms, forums, and pulpits can be battlegrounds for justice. That when people speak out—when they demand change—the echoes can last for generations.

Of course, not everyone welcomed this shift. In 1834, shortly after the debates, Lane's board of trustees—gripped by fear of controversy—moved to stifle the growing abolitionist movement within the school. Instead of bowing to the restrictions, students and faculty staged a mass exodus, forming a group that history now remembers as the "Lane Rebels." These young radicals carried the fire of abolitionism with them, fueling the movement in ways that would forever alter the course of history.

Now, let's be real for a moment. What if I, as a modern-day Black man, had been thrown into those debates? Imagine me time-traveling back to the 1830s, armed with everything I know now. It would be like someone trying to convince me to ditch my iPhone and go back to a flip phone. I mean, sure, in a museum, it's cool to look at. But to actually go back and live in that time? To hear people argue about whether or not I am worthy of freedom, as if that is even up for debate? It's not exactly the kind of nostalgic throwback I'd sign up for.

Still, Lane Seminary's place in the abolitionist movement remains one of the most crucial chapters in the fight against slavery. Its influence stretched beyond the school itself, intertwining with the work of Underground Railroad leaders in Cincinnati's free Black communities. While there's little direct evidence that the seminary itself was an active stop on the Underground Railroad, its students were undeniably part of the network that helped enslaved people reach freedom.

But as history marched forward, the home that once served as a stage for these bold debates changed hands. In 1865, just as the Civil War drew to a close, Joseph G. Monfort purchased what is now known as the Harriet Beecher Stowe House. Over the next few decades, the house evolved. The remaining sections of the back verandah were enclosed, and by 1908, the home underwent a major transformation—out went the original staircase, replaced by the grand one that still stands today. The room that now houses the bookstore was added, as were new mantels and thin oak flooring.

For generations, the Monfort family occupied the home, adding their own layers to its history. But by the late 1920s, the last Monfort resident,

Mary Monfort, moved out, leaving the house on the verge of yet another reinvention.

And that's the thing about history—these places don't just disappear. They evolve. They shift, change, and continue to hold echoes of the past. Lane Seminary may be long gone, but its legacy, its debates, and the voices that once filled its halls? They still resonate. And if we listen closely, they still have something to teach us.

THE FORMER BEECHER FAMILY HOME BECOMES THE EDGEMONT INN

By the 1930s and 1940s, this home had stepped into yet another chapter, this time as a Black-owned boardinghouse and tavern known as the Edgemont Inn, under the management of Irene Bacon, and a place listed in *The Green Book*, a vital guide that helped Black travelers navigate America's racial barriers, offering them safety, dignity, and a warm meal when the road was anything but welcoming.

And if *The Green Book* doesn't ring a bell, maybe you can recall the 2018 Oscar-winning film of the same name, starring Mahershala Ali and Viggo Mortensen.[30] It reimagines the classic road trip story, except this one is set in the Deep South during Jim Crow. Picture a refined, classically trained Black pianist forced to rely on his tough, no-frills Italian American driver to get him from one venue to the next without running into trouble. Think *The Odd Couple* meets *Driving Miss Daisy*, with Mortensen tearing through buckets of fried chicken while Ali does his best to keep his composure. But beneath the humor and the clash of personalities, the film—like the original *Green Book* itself—reminds us just how vital safe havens like the Edgemont Inn were for Black travelers navigating a country that often refused to see their humanity.

But let's get back on track.

By the 1930s, Cincinnati's Walnut Hills neighborhood, home to the Stowe House, had grown into a thriving Black business district, pulsing with the energy of entrepreneurs, artists, and community leaders shaping their own futures. The house itself had evolved into a boardinghouse and tavern. Not just any tavern, the Edgemont Inn was a beacon of safety in a time when Black travelers couldn't take something as simple as lodging for granted.

That's where *The Green Book* came in. Created in 1936 by Victor Hugo Green, this travel guide was more than just a list of hotels and restaurants; it

Left: *The Green Book*, developed by Victor Hugo Green in 1936 for Black motorists. *Harriet Beecher Stowe House.*

Below: The Edgemont Inn. *Harriet Beecher Stowe House.*

was a survival tool. Black motorists crisscrossing a deeply segregated America needed to know where they could stop without facing humiliation—or worse. What started as a New York City–focused guide soon expanded to include locations across the country, listing businesses that welcomed Black patrons, offering them not only shelter but also a sense of dignity.

By 1940, the Edgemont Inn, formerly the Stowe House, had secured its place in *The Green Book*, standing as one of Cincinnati's few safe taverns for the Black community. The first floor was home to a lively tavern, a social hub where stories were swapped, ideas debated, and plans for progress made. Upstairs, Mrs. Irene Bacon, a Black woman with an eye for business and a heart for community, ran the boardinghouse, providing weary travelers with a safe place to rest.

But this wasn't just a stopover; it was a landmark. A century earlier, Harriet Beecher Stowe's family called this house home, a space where abolitionist ideals were nurtured and challenged. Now, as the Edgemont Inn, it carried that same spirit forward, offering a haven for Black travelers and a gathering place for those continuing the fight for freedom in a new era. The struggle had changed, but the need for safe spaces—and the power of community—remained as urgent as ever.

So, this historic home has stood the test of time, not just as a house but also as a living, breathing time capsule. It's a place where every creaky floorboard hums with the echoes of those who've walked before and where the walls, if they could talk, might just sigh and say, "Y'all wouldn't believe the things I've seen." Or, as my Aunt Sarah liked to put it, "These walls have heard so much, they probably need a vacation."

But beneath the charm and character, this space holds something deeper—a legacy of resilience. It wasn't just a stopover; it was a stronghold for social change, a safehouse where Black leaders could gather, strategize, and simply exist in a world that often denied them that right. And even now, we're still uncovering just how this space nurtured movements, fueled conversations, and stood as a quiet but steadfast witness to history in the making.

7

The Margaret Garner Story

I've always been drawn to contests—the kind where the odds are stacked high and the underdogs refuse to back down. There's something about the struggle, the sheer defiance of expectation, that hooks me. Maybe that's why I become glued to *The Amazing Race*, *American Idol*, and every breathtaking moment of the Summer Olympics, cheering for the ones no one thought could win. Because I know what it feels like to be underestimated.

I remember sitting in my high school guidance counselor's office, the air thick with the unspoken limits they had already placed on me. "You're not advanced placement material," they said, with the kind of certainty that was supposed to close the door on any dreams I might've had. But instead of shutting me down, it lit a fire. I wasn't just going to prove them wrong—I was going to rewrite the whole damn script. The classroom became my battleground, my late-night study sessions a rebellion. Every fact I memorized, every formula I mastered felt like a weapon in a war I hadn't chosen but was determined to win.

If there's any group that knows the weight of fighting against the odds, it's Black America. Our very existence has been a battle, a long, relentless push against a country built on systems meant to keep us caged. I grew up hearing stories of that struggle, passed down like sacred scripture. But there's one story that sticks with me, not just for what it revealed but for how it found me—unexpected, almost absurd in its timing.

It was 1987, a year when the world felt like it was on fire—an Amtrak crash, the Iran-Contra scandal, the Unabomber, Black Monday wiping out fortunes overnight. Somewhere in that chaos, a story crossed my path, and I never let go.

Back then, I was just a nerdy Black boy, teetering between the third and fourth grade, still figuring out where I fit in the world. But that was the year it really sank in—I wasn't just a kid. I was a Black kid, moving through a country that already saw me as a threat before I even knew what danger looked like. While other kids were caught up in Michael Jordan dropping 58 points for the Bulls, I was waking up to something heavier.

We had just moved to the Westside of Covington, Kentucky—Cincinnati's quieter, southern shadow. My mom made sure we landed in a part of the neighborhood with Black residents, a place where we could breathe without the constant weight of white stares. It was a neighborhood stitched together by kinship, lifelong acquaintances and distant cousins who were all family. That summer, all I could talk about was riding The Vortex at Kings Island, my mouth running a mile a minute about how I'd be the first one to brave the loops. But beyond my little world of roller coasters and childhood bravado, something seismic was happening.

That was the year Toni Morrison gave the world *Beloved*, a story that felt like history reaching out with blood on its hands, whispering truths we weren't supposed to forget. Sethe, a woman who had known the shackles of slavery, made an unthinkable choice: to take her own daughter's life rather than let her be dragged back into bondage. It's a story too devastating to be fiction—because it isn't.

And that was the weight I was just beginning to understand, that Black history isn't just something you read in books. It's something that lives inside you, shaping the way you move, the way you dream, the way you fight.

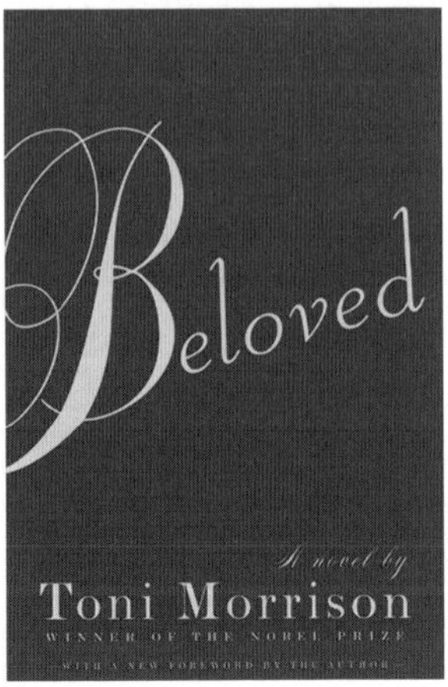

Beloved was the first of Morrison's novels to pull us deep into history, planting us firmly in the years after the Civil War—long enough for the wounds of slavery to fester but not nearly long enough for them to heal. Nearly two decades had passed since Sethe made the unthinkable choice to take her own child's life rather than see her dragged back into the nightmare of bondage. Now, she's in Cincinnati, living with Denver, the daughter she was still carrying when she made her desperate escape from Kentucky. They've built a life, quiet and fragile, but one day, a strange young woman appears at their

Opposite: *Beloved* book cover. *Above*: Toni Morrison. *Smithsonian*.

doorstep. She barely speaks, barely explains, but she calls herself Beloved. And from the moment she crosses the threshold, she consumes Sethe and Denver, settling into their home, their hearts, their very sense of reality in ways none of them are ready for.

That's Morrison's power. She doesn't just tell a story; she pulls you into it, makes you feel the weight of its ghosts, the echoes of a past that refuses to stay buried. Her genius was recognized in so many ways, but when President Obama placed the Presidential Medal of Freedom around her neck in

2012,[31] it was a full-circle moment—a nation honoring a woman who had spent her career forcing it to reckon with its past. Her brilliance with *Beloved* even led to the 1998 film adaptation, brought to life by Jonathan Demme, with Oprah Winfrey stepping into Sethe's tortured, determined shoes.

But before we get into the real-life horror that inspired *Beloved*, let's step back. What was the world like in Sethe's time? What kind of country made her choice even imaginable?

The 1850s arrived in a whirlwind. Millard Fillmore took over as the thirteenth president of the United States after Zachary Taylor's sudden death in 1850,[32] and the country was shifting fast. In the North, industrialization was booming. Railroads and telegraph lines stretched across states, connecting cities, fueling economies, and pulling in waves of European immigrants looking for work and land. The nation was modernizing, pushing forward at a relentless pace.

But down south, progress meant something entirely different. There, the economy still ran on human suffering. With the soil of the Southeast exhausted from generations of plantation farming, enslavers were moving their "property" westward, staking new claims on the fertile cotton lands of the Southwest. Black bodies remained the foundation of Southern wealth, shackled to a system that refused to die.

Then came 1850, the year the government tried to put a lid on the growing tensions with the so-called Compromise of 1850. But one piece of that deal, the Fugitive Slave Act, was gasoline on an already burning fire. It gave enslavers the right to hunt down escaped enslaved people anywhere in the country and drag them back into bondage no matter how far they had run. Even free Black people in the North lived in fear, knowing that their freedom was as fragile as a piece of paper or the word of a white man who claimed otherwise.

The outrage was instant. It spread like wildfire, and among those who refused to look away was Harriet Beecher Stowe. In 1852, she put pen to paper and gave the world *Uncle Tom's Cabin*, a novel that shattered illusions and exposed the brutality of slavery in ways that made it impossible to ignore. It wasn't just a story—it was a reckoning.

So was *Beloved*. Morrison, like Stowe before her, knew that history isn't just something we remember. It's something we carry. It haunts us, shapes us, and sometimes, if we're brave enough to face it, it can even set us free.

During the brutal era of American slavery, resistance was a necessity. Survival meant fighting in ways that history often struggles to comprehend. Two haunting themes rise from those dark years: the desperate flights toward freedom and the gut-wrenching act of infanticide. Enslaved men and women, driven by a hunger for liberation that no chain could break, risked everything to escape to the North, hoping to find safety, dignity, and a future beyond servitude. But alongside those acts of courage was a far more devastating reality—the impossible decision some enslaved mothers made to take their children's lives rather than watch them be swallowed by a world built on their suffering.

Then came the law that changed everything: the Fugitive Slave Act, passed on September 18, 1850. It was a weapon, a federal decree that stripped the North of its status as a haven and turned free soil into hunting grounds. Rooted in two earlier laws that allowed for the capture and return of runaway enslaved people, this act emboldened slave catchers, sending them deep into states that had long been seen as beacons of hope.

Even before this, the fight over slavery had been brewing. The Fugitive Slave Clause had been baked into the U.S. Constitution, but by the late 1780s and early 1790s, antislavery sentiment was gaining momentum in the North. Calls to dismantle the institution grew louder, forcing Congress to respond—not by ending slavery but by tightening its grip. The Fugitive Slave Act of 1793 gave local governments the power to seize and return escapees, threatening harsh penalties for anyone who dared to help them. But resistance was strong, and by 1850, Congress escalated its efforts. This new law wasn't just stricter—it was ruthless. It made it easier than ever for enslavers to track down runaways, and it criminalized anyone who dared to stand in their way.

This was war in the halls of Congress. Southern lawmakers pushed hard for the 1793 act, arguing that the fight over slavery was driving a wedge between the states. By the time the 1850 law was passed, the divide was undeniable, and tensions were boiling over. But what did that look like here, in Northern Kentucky, where the Ohio River was the thin, dangerous line between bondage and freedom?

That's where Gaines Tavern comes in—a not-so-little establishment in Boone County that, in the early 1800s, stood at the crossroads of commerce, politics, and the brutal realities of slavery. Built in 1814 by Abner Gaines, the tavern sat along the Cincinnati-Lexington Turnpike, a major artery for travelers moving between the North and South. This wasn't just a resting place for weary souls; it was a hub where deals were made, power was brokered, and history was written in ways most would rather forget. Auctions were held here, business was conducted, and men in positions of power gathered to shape the future of Boone County.

Abner Gaines himself was more than just a tavern owner. Born in 1787, he was a lawyer, politician, land speculator, and businessman who left his mark on Kentucky. He served in both the House of Representatives and the Senate, influencing legislation that shaped the region well into the nineteenth century.[33] By the time he passed away in 1857, his legacy was cemented. But the stories of the enslaved people who lived, labored, and suffered in places like Gaines Tavern? Those are the stories that history tried to silence. And those are the stories we need to remember.

And then there's Margaret Garner—a name that still haunts history—a woman whose desperate choice shattered the nation's illusions about slavery. In 1856, she did what so many enslaved people only dreamed of: she ran.[34] With her family by her side, she crossed the icy Ohio River, leaving behind the Kentucky plantation where she had known nothing but bondage. But when recapture became inevitable, Margaret made a decision so devastating, so gut-wrenching, that it still echoes today: she would rather see her children dead than condemned to a life in chains.

Margaret's story wasn't just another fugitive slave narrative. It was proof of how brutal, how unforgiving, and how inescapable slavery was. Her act of defiance shocked the nation and forced people to confront the horrifying truth: If a mother believed death was kinder than life in slavery, what did that say about the system America was built on? Her story inspired books, plays, and even operas, a lasting testament to a time many have tried to forget.

Born into slavery in Kentucky around 1834, Margaret Garner knew only captivity. But in January 1856, she and her family made their daring escape, slipping across the frozen Ohio River into Cincinnati. For a moment, freedom felt possible. They hid in the home of a formerly enslaved man, while others in their group managed to continue their journey north, toward Canada and true liberation. But Margaret's freedom lasted mere hours. Slave catchers, backed by U.S. Marshals tracked them down with ruthless precision, storming the house in a violent raid.

And that's when Margaret made the choice that would define her legacy. She would not let her children be dragged back into the hell she had fought to escape. In an act of unimaginable anguish, she grabbed a butcher knife and killed her two-year-old daughter. She attempted to take the lives of her other children before she was stopped. It was not just an act of resistance; it was a mother's final, desperate attempt to reclaim power in a world that had stolen everything from her.

Her arrest set off one of the most infamous legal battles of the era. Was Margaret a person, capable of being charged with murder? Or was she

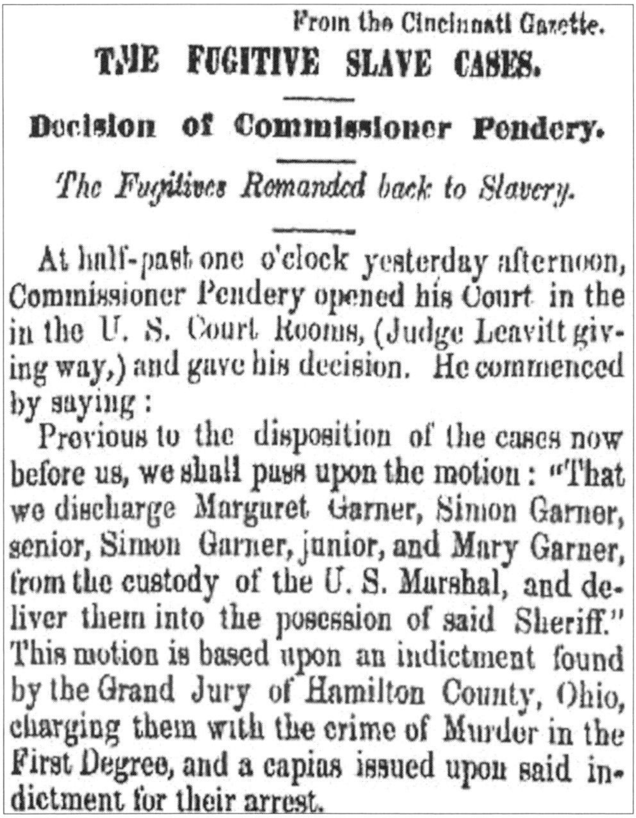

From the Cincinnati Gazette.

THE FUGITIVE SLAVE CASES.

Decision of Commissioner Pendery.

The Fugitives Remanded back to Slavery.

At half-past one o'clock yesterday afternoon, Commissioner Pendery opened his Court in the in the U. S. Court Rooms, (Judge Leavitt giving way,) and gave his decision. He commenced by saying:

Previous to the disposition of the cases now before us, we shall pass upon the motion: "That we discharge Marguret Garner, Simon Garner, senior, Simon Garner, junior, and Mary Garner, from the custody of the U. S. Marshal, and deliver them into the posession of said Sheriff." This motion is based upon an indictment found by the Grand Jury of Hamilton County, Ohio, charging them with the crime of Murder in the First Degree, and a capias issued upon said indictment for their arrest.

"The Fugitive Slave Cases," *Daily Cleveland* (OH) *Herald*, February 28, 1856.

merely property, to be returned to her enslaver under the Fugitive Slave Law? Her lawyer fought to have her tried under Ohio law, arguing that as a free state, it had jurisdiction over her actions. But the slave catchers, backed by her so-called owner, pushed for federal law to prevail. The stakes were as high as they came: freedom versus bondage, humanity versus property, justice versus a system built to deny it.

In the end, the system won. Margaret was sent back into slavery, her surviving children forced to endure the very life she had tried to save them from. Yet her story refused to be buried. It became a rallying cry, a terrifying glimpse into the reality of a country at war with its own morality. Because if death seemed like the lesser evil, what did that say about the world she was trying to escape?

But let's pause for a moment. What if Margaret's choice, tragic as it was, was also a form of resistance? I know it's hard to think about, but conceptualizing infanticide this way gives those enslaved mothers their agency. It frames their decision as an act of defiance, an insurrection against a system that gave them no way out.

Infanticide, in all its horror, became a desperate and harrowing form of resistance during slavery. These enslaved mothers, staring down the unbearable future their children would face, made the choice that death was better than a lifetime in chains. It was an unimaginable decision, but in it was a defiance so deep and so personal that it refused to let their children be reduced to property. In these tragic acts, these mothers made a powerful statement: they would not let their babies be subjugated, not if they could help it.

Margaret Garner's story, and others like hers, serve as painful reminders of the cruelty of slavery. But they also highlight the unimaginable choices that people had to make and the resilience it took to resist, even in the most heart-wrenching ways.

Margaret Garner's case ignited a nationwide debate, forcing the country to confront the ugly truth of slavery and the treatment of enslaved people. For some, her actions were a desperate, heartbreaking response to an unbearable system. Others saw her as nothing more than a murderer. But Margaret never got her day in court. She died in jail from typhoid fever before the trial could take place.

Her defense attorney had one last hope, a legal gamble that could have changed everything. He pushed for Margaret to be charged with murder, not because he wanted to see her punished, but because it meant her case would be tried in Ohio, a free state. If he could get her into the hands of Ohio's legal system, there was a chance the governor would intervene, issue a pardon, and set her free. It was a bold, high-stakes strategy, and the entire country was watching.

But the law was never designed to work in Margaret's favor. The judge ruled that federal law overruled state law, and just like that, she was ripped from Ohio's grasp and handed back to her enslaver in Kentucky. Ohio authorities weren't willing to let her go without a fight; they issued an extradition warrant, attempting to bring her back to face murder charges in a state that at least acknowledged her humanity. But her enslaver knew the risks. He kept her moving, shuttling her from place to place, ensuring she stayed just beyond reach.

During the long, cruel stretch of extradition, tragedy struck once more. Margaret, already robbed of so much, found herself aboard a vessel bound for the South when disaster came swiftly. The ship she was on collided with another, the impact throwing bodies into the chaotic waters. In the frenzy,

Margaret was cast overboard, swallowed by the same river she had once crossed in search of freedom.

Yet they said she did not fight, did not struggle, did not scream for rescue. Instead, she exuded relief, perhaps even peace. Because Margaret Garner had long understood a truth too unbearable to speak: in a world where slavery reigned, death could be the only true deliverance. She had already tried to spare her children the horrors she knew too well. Now, the river, vast and indifferent, offered her an escape of her own. She tried to let it take her, tried to follow the child she had lost. But the world was not done with her suffering just yet. Rough hands dragged her from the depths, forcing her to endure once more the life she had spent every breath trying to escape.

After that, Margaret faded from history. No more courtrooms. No more headlines. No more defiant acts that would make her name echo through time.

But in the autumn of 1870, the *Cincinnati Chronicle* sat down with Robert Garner, Margaret's husband, the man who had survived it all. Five years had passed since the war had ended, since the legal chains of slavery had been broken. Robert, now an aging man, lived with his two grown sons. But Margaret was not there. Her absence, heavy and unspoken, lingered like a shadow over his weary frame.

Robert had fought for the Union during the war, taking up arms against the very system that had once enslaved him. But even in victory, his battle had not ended. He carried a story not often told, one steeped in suffering, survival, and the relentless cruelty of fate. He recounted how, after their infamous trial, he and Margaret had been sent south, forced into servitude in New Orleans. What began as household labor soon descended into something far worse. Judge Dewitt Clinton Bonham saw them not as people but profit, purchasing the couple and condemning them to the backbreaking existence of plantation life in Tennessee Landing, Mississippi.

And there, beneath the unrelenting Mississippi sun, Robert's world shattered. In 1858, Margaret, his wife, his partner in resistance, his tether to a love that had endured the unimaginable, was taken by typhoid fever. She had survived the river, only to be claimed by disease, her spirit finally escaping the way her body never could.[35]

Robert carried the weight of that loss for the rest of his days. Though he had outlived slavery and fought for the freedom of others, true freedom—freedom with Margaret by his side—was never his to have.

His own journey ended quietly in 1871. A shipboard injury, a chest wound that never quite healed, likely claimed his life. No great monument was built in his honor. No grand obituary marked his passing. If he was buried in

Cincinnati, it was most likely in a potter's field, laid to rest among those the world too often forgets.

But history refused to forget Margaret Garner. Her name became more than a tragedy, transforming into a warning, a reckoning, a wound on the conscience of a nation. Her case ignited a firestorm, turning the Fugitive Slave Act into a battleground for justice. The choices she was forced to make—the unthinkable, the unbearable—were immortalized in poetry, literature, and whispered remembrance.

It was her suffering, her defiance, her desperate act of resistance that inspired Frances Harper to write her haunting 1859 poem "Slave Mother: A Tale of Ohio." And long after the river let Margaret go, her story remained, refusing to be silenced.

Margaret's story is a wound in history, a painful, necessary reminder of a past too many try to soften. But there was no softening the world she lived in, no comfort in the chains she fought so hard to break. And maybe, just maybe, that's why her story still lingers. Because it forces us to ask: What would you have done if you were her?

Margaret Garner's story is more than a tragedy; it's a reflection of countless untold histories that quietly shape the landscape of greater Cincinnati. Her desperate act, as horrifying as it was, didn't come from cruelty. It came from an unshakable love, a mother's last defense against a world built to destroy her children. It forces us to confront a brutal truth: for the enslaved, even the most unthinkable choices were born from the depths of resistance.

Her story, though heavy with sorrow, is not an isolated one. It is stitched into the fabric of Cincinnati's past, woven into the legacy of Black men and women who defied oppression, who built lives, communities, and movements despite the forces set against them. These stories, often buried beneath the grand narratives of the city's rise, are the true foundation of its greatness. They are testaments to the resilience, ingenuity, and strength of those who fought for a future beyond bondage.

To acknowledge Margaret's story is not just to recount history; it's to hold ourselves accountable. It's to ask the hard questions. What do we do with this knowledge? How do we honor not just her suffering but also her defiance?

Acknowledgment alone isn't justice. We must go further.

First, we must educate. The truth of Margaret's life and the countless others like hers must be told in our schools, ensuring that future generations understand the weight of history, not just as a record of the past but also as a guide for the future. By fostering awareness, we build empathy, and through empathy, we cultivate change.

Second, we must advocate. The past teaches us that laws have always shaped who is seen as fully human and who is not. We must push for stronger legal protections, not just in memory of those who suffered but also for the marginalized communities still fighting for recognition, dignity, and justice today.

And finally, we must heal. The wounds of history do not fade on their own. They demand care. That means supporting survivors of violence and systemic oppression, funding mental healthcare, investing in communities, and creating spaces where truth is spoken and justice is pursued with real action.

Margaret's story did not vanish into history's shadow. It has endured. It lives on in Toni Morrison's *Beloved*, a novel that gives breath to her pain and power. It echoes in the artifacts that remain, fragments of a life that remind us of the journey she took and the forces she fought against.

But most importantly, her story lives in us. In our reckoning with the past. In our responsibility to the present. And in our commitment to shaping a future where no mother, no child, no person is ever forced to make the choice Margaret did.

Sweet Home/Maplewood

Abner Gaines and his wife, Elizabeth Matthews, raised thirteen children—a lineage that stretched across the young nation, leaving a trail of prominence, power, and paradox. Their eldest, James Matthews Gaines, became the first postmaster of the settlement once called Gaines Cross Roads, what we now know as Walton, Kentucky, back in 1815, binding the family's name to Kentucky soil. Woodford Gaines traded the quiet of home for military order, serving as a paymaster at Fort Smith, Arkansas, while his brother Richard found favor with President Andrew Jackson himself, who appointed him U.S. district attorney of Mississippi.

Legrand Gaines pursued fortune in the Deep South, building wealth as a cotton planter near New Orleans. Benjamin Gaines, too, found his empire in the soil, owning vast plantations in Chicot County, Arkansas. William H. Gaines staked his claim at Hot Springs, Arkansas, and won, a portion of that healing land now tied forever to his name.

Then came Major John Pollard Gaines—soldier, statesman, and the original owner of Maplewood Farm, where Margaret Garner and her family were enslaved. Before his departure to the Oregon Territory to serve as governor, John sold the farm to his brother, Archibald. It was Archibald K. Gaines whose name would become infamous in American history as the man from whom Margaret Garner fled, whose pursuit led to one of the most haunting trials of the nineteenth century and who was said to be the father of several of her children.

The name Archibald Gaines lingers in the air like a ghost, heavy with the weight of a history most would rather forget. Boone County, Kentucky, holds its share of dark truths, and Maplewood—his sprawling estate—was more than a plantation. It was a world built on bondage, its foundation laid by the hands of men and women who had no claim to their own lives, yet they carried within them the quiet, unbreakable will to survive.

If the name doesn't immediately send a chill down your spine, perhaps Morrison's words will. She renamed it in *Beloved*, transforming Maplewood into something more hauntingly familiar—Sweet Home. But the bones of that story weren't born from fiction. They were carved from the real suffering, the real resilience, the real people who lived and labored under Gaines' rule. Morrison resurrected the past and breathed into it the pain, the hope, the desperation, and the fleeting moments of humanity that existed even in the cruelest of spaces.

For Sethe and the others, Sweet Home was a contradiction—both shelter and cage, the site of unspeakable horrors and the fragile place where love still dared to exist. Morrison captured that tension in a way that feels almost tangible, as if the trees themselves whisper of lives stolen and dreams deferred. But in Boone County, there is no need for imagination. Maplewood was real. The people who walked its grounds, who bore its weight, who longed for something beyond its reach—they were real, too.

Today, there is little left of Maplewood. Time has swallowed most of it, as if trying to erase what once stood. All that remains is a single structure—the kitchen, a lone witness to a world that no longer exists but refuses to be forgotten. Within those walls, food was prepared for the Gaines family, but it was also the space where the enslaved stood, worked, and withstood. It is the last remnant of their presence, a quiet, stubborn testament to lives history tried to silence. And like Sweet Home, it is a reminder that even in the deepest shadows of oppression, people dared to dream of something more.

The Gaines Tavern

Gaines Tavern still stands in Boone County, Kentucky, a quiet structure with a deafening past. Built in the early 1800s, it was more than just a rest stop for weary travelers; it was a monument to power, a place where wealth and status were built on the backs of the enslaved. For the Gaines family, it was a symbol of privilege. For those in bondage, it was just another reminder that freedom was always just out of reach. And looming over it all was Archibald Gaines, the same man whose name is forever tied to Maplewood plantation—the same place where Margaret Garner's tragic and defiant story unfolded.

Gaines wasn't just a landowner; he was an architect of suffering, a man who thrived under a system that denied others their humanity. Among those enslaved at Maplewood was Margaret Garner, a woman whose name history refuses to forget. In 1856, she and her family made a desperate run for freedom, fleeing across the frozen Ohio River toward the promise of something more. But when capture became inevitable, Margaret made a decision that still reverberates through time—she chose to end her daughter's life rather than see her forced back into slavery. It was an unspeakable tragedy, but it was also an act of resistance that forced

Gaines Tavern, Abner Gaines home. *Kenton County Public Library*.

the nation to confront the brutality of its own laws. Her story became a rallying cry, fueling the abolitionist movement and forever etching her name into the painful narrative of American history.

The connection between Gaines Tavern and Maplewood is unshakable. The two sites are bound together by the weight of oppression, both tied to a man whose wealth was built on the suffering of others. Today, the tavern remains standing, a historical landmark. Maplewood, however, has all but disappeared, leaving only its kitchen behind as the last witness to what once was. But buildings are not the true markers of history—people are. And the lives lived, the pain endured, and the resistance waged within those walls remind us that we cannot separate the structures from the stories they hold. To understand our past, we must be willing to confront it, to acknowledge the truth that lingers in the echoes of Margaret Garner's name.

THE MODERN MEDEA

Modern Medea stands as one of the few tangible echoes of Margaret Garner's harrowing story, a haunting testament to a moment that shook the conscience of a nation. Created by artist Thomas Satterwhite Noble,[36] the painting doesn't just depict history; it forces you to confront it.

At its center, Margaret stands frozen in time, her face etched with a grief too deep for words. To her right, her child lies motionless on the floor, a life stolen by a mother's desperate attempt to save her from a fate worse than death. On the left, two white men recoil in horror, one pointing in shock, their expressions twisted in disbelief. But what are they truly appalled by—the act itself or the unbearable truth it exposes? That a mother, faced with the certainty of her child's return to bondage, believed death was the only mercy left?

Noble's brushstrokes do more than capture a tragic moment; they peel back the layers of race, gender, and identity, demanding that we examine the stories we tell ourselves about power, justice, and who gets to decide the value of a life. *Modern Medea* isn't just a painting; it's an unflinching mirror, daring us to look into its depths and ask ourselves whether we are still haunted by the same injustices Margaret fought against.

The Modern Medea. Encyclopedia of Arkansas.

Historic Marker

In 1990, the Kentucky Historical Society and the Kentucky Department of Highways placed a marker in Covington, Kentucky. It's a simple slab of metal and words, yet it carries the weight of a history too heavy to ignore. It stands in honor of Margaret Garner, a woman whose life was defined by the brutal reality of slavery and the desperate, unimaginable choices made in pursuit of freedom.

Positioned near the very land where Margaret's fateful journey began, the marker is a permanent reminder of a past that still lingers in the bones of this country. Her story is one of defiance and devastation, a testament to both the resilience of the enslaved and the horrifying depths of the system that bound them. To stand before it is to feel the echoes of history, to reckon with the painful truth that, for some, freedom was worth any cost—even the unthinkable.

Margaret Garner historical marker (Covington, Kentucky). *Historical Marker Database.*

It challenges us to see beyond dates and plaques, to confront the raw humanity within the larger historical narrative. It stands as both a tribute and a warning, proof that the struggle for dignity and justice has never been a passive one. It was fought for, bled for, and, in Margaret's case, mourned in ways too complex for history books to fully contain.

Conclusion

I am the direct descendant of enslaved individuals. And I don't say that lightly. I mean, I do have dark skin and I am living here in the United States, but I could be a descendant of dark-skinned people from other areas of the world who were not enslaved here in the United States.

We descendants of the enslaved occupy an awkward space here in America. Our families most likely did not choose to come to this country, and no, our families did not choose to stay in this country—with the whole "being forced to work for white people" and all. But our families did decide to stay in this country once they were emancipated. And why wouldn't they? It's not like they could easily carve out their space back in Africa once they were set free. I could see my great-great-grandfather, once he was set free, showing up on the doorstep of his long-lost relatives in Africa and saying, "Hey, family! I'm home!"

The emancipated members of my family traveled from the southern parts of Kentucky, Tennessee, and Georgia to Northern Kentucky in the hopes of finding equality, and over a century later, I feel like we are still looking for it. I mean, come on, how rare is it, still, to have a piece of infrastructure, like a bridge or a highway, named after a Black person?

When I was a child growing up in Covington, Kentucky, living almost in the shadow of Cincinnati, Ohio, in the 1980s and 1990s, my mother acted as a cloak, protecting me from much of the ugliness and racism my great-great-grandfather attempted to escape from in the South. But like many Black mothers, she was only able to shield her Black son for so long.

Growing up as a Black male in Northern Kentucky, a region that has, according to the U.S. census, a modest Black population of roughly 5 to 7 percent, presented unique challenges and opportunities. This area, nestled at the crossroads of Midwest cultures and Southern influences, offered a distinct blend of small-town charm and urban proximity. The rich tapestry of the region's history and the resilience of its people created a narrative that was both compelling and deeply rooted in a sense of community. This area, often overshadowed by the bustling city of Cincinnati, Ohio, and nearly forgotten by the broader state of Kentucky, shaped my Black experience in a profound way. Navigating a landscape where my presence was sometimes overlooked required resilience, strength, and a deep sense of identity.

While I was growing up, we lived in Covington's predominantly white Westside neighborhood. But in the part of the neighborhood where we lived, there was a cluster of Black residents. Even in the 1980s, realtors were still nudging Black families to buy homes where there were already other Black families. So much for desegregation, am I right? You see, before settling into the home where I would spend my formative years, my mom and stepdad at the time, looked at two other houses, both in white neighborhoods in the city. Thinking back, I can't really be sure that the reason we settled on the house that we did was because my mom thought that living next to other Black folks would be better for her family *or* if the realtor said something like, "Oh, there are other Black families there. I think you will fit in much better there." I have made a mental note to get the down-low from my mom the next time that I see her.

While living in this house, I spent many days after school and on the weekends at the local Boys and Girls Club. Yes, I pride myself with being among the many famous and talented who crafted their childhood at the Club, along with Denzel Washing and Jenifer Lopez—not to name drop or anything. The Club was not only a fun place for me, but it was also cheap childcare for my mom. I mean, at the time, annual memberships cost like five bucks a year, and you could go there after school until 8:00 p.m. In the summer, you could go to the Club during the daytime while your parents were at work. My mom made sure me and all three of my younger brothers were card-carrying members.

That was my childhood. I was either at school, at the Club, or playing tag football with friends on the city streets—or, in the summer, at the pool in Randolph Park in Covington's Eastside neighborhood, the city's predominantly Black neighborhood. One year, when I was in grade school,

Kareem A. Simpson's childhood home, 216 West Fifteenth Street, Covington, Kentucky. *K.A. Simpson Collection.*

I asked my mom why we were going way across town to the Randolph Park pool when we could go to Goebel Park pool in Covington's Mainstrasse neighborhood, which was just as close but in the white neighborhood. "Baby," my mom started to say as she took me in her arms, "for people who look like us, there are just places that are safer for us not to go."

I was a nerdy kid, book smarts mostly, and I could hold my own with basic and even higher-level comprehension, so her message got to me loud and clear. But this was also about the time that I began seeing things outside my mom's sphere of influence were different for people who looked like me.

This was about the same time that I was first called the N-word. I couldn't have been more than six or seven years old. I was in the car with my mom, and she was trying to switch lanes on a city street in Covington, probably running late for something or another or trying to rush back home. It seemed as though the driver just to the left and slightly positioned behind my mom's rear bumper was going to let her over because he had stopped his car with enough room to let her in, so we attempted to change lanes. At that very moment, he pulled ahead, causing my mother to swerve almost onto the sidewalk shoulder of the street.

Kareem A. Simpson sits for a photoshoot in the Modeling Club at the (then) Kenton County Boys and Girls Club, circa 1990. *Jacqueline Pierce Photography.*

As he pulled ahead of us, the driver honked his horn and yelled out through his open window the N-word. And then he immediately sped off ahead of us. Even at that age, I knew what that word meant. I also knew what that word, when heard, should have made me feel. I mean, I can only imagine what you are feeling as you learn that I was called the N-word. No, I did not feel that rage that I thought I would. I felt empowered. I felt this way because this man, this white man, was so afraid of my mother and I that he almost hit another car while he sped away from us. I guess he was afraid of us. Ignorance will do that to you, I guess—make you afraid and do and say stupid things.

But this was the first instance of many in my life in which my skin color made me look scarier than I really was, seem like more of a threat than I really am. Like that time in high school when the school counselor took umbrage when I asked to be placed in advanced placement classes. I was transferring from a private, college prep school, where I skipped the seventh and eighth grades, into the local public school. "It just doesn't look as though you can handle the work," the counselor said.

Or how about the time, just a few years ago, when I was a bartender at a local bar in Covington. I was outside in the back alleyway of the bar, on break, when two police officers drove up to me in their squad car, headlights positioned on me. The two officers got out and asked me for identification. Unfortunately, I did not have my ID on me because it was in my work bag inside the bar. After taking my social security number and running it through their database for any warrants, the other officer went into my place of work to verify that I, in fact, was employed there. After they found no warrants

Kareem A. Simpson's family *(from left to right)* Aderemi Giwa (brother), Adeniyi Giwa (brother), Adeshina Giwa (brother), and Lillian Simpson (grandmother). *K.A. Simpson Collection.*

and verified my employment, the officers said I was free to return to work. I must have looked real scary standing outside drinking Coca-Cola.

I won't even tell you about the myriad other times that I've been eyeballed while walking into a clothing store or how many times a salesman shrank away from me when I walked onto a car lot. I know that it sounds cliché, but that is life when you have darker skin like mine in America.

It doesn't matter that I once served as a noncommissioned officer in the Military Intelligence Branch of the United States Army. It doesn't matter that I can hold a conversation with you in Korean or French, depending on what type of restaurant I am in. Before I open my mouth to speak, I am still seen as a poor, uneducated threat just because of the color of my skin. If I had a dollar for every time someone said to me, after an initial conversation, "You speak so well," I would be a millionaire by now.

Sadly, this type of negative prejudice just doesn't hurt people's feelings or make them want to throw their newspaper on the floor when they hear about injustices. Wait, who reads physical newspapers anymore? This prejudice has permeated our country and is wrecking the very fabric that holds our society together. It's manifesting in the worst way, by killing Black men—and sometimes Black boys.

And just with ongoing police-involved incidents, we find ourselves, once again, trying to understand how misconceptions and misunderstandings can lead to multiple deaths and a nation saddled with grief and outrage. (And my white friends think I'm overly nervous when a cop pulls up behind me while I'm driving.)

But despite this, I know that police officers are the backbone of our community, and there is no doubt that those who serve in this role have an exceedingly difficult and highly honorable job. Their split-second decisions could dictate whether a woman is murdered, a child is abducted, an elderly resident's property is vandalized, or a lone gunman commits mass murder.

NKY Black Lives Matter March (June 2020). *K.A. Simpson Collection.*

I may be a little apprehensive when I see that cruiser growing larger in my rear-view mirror, but I know that we need police officers in our society and we want them to protect and serve.

Because of this, we grant officers the right to "protect and serve." But there are officers who abuse the power we give them, and far too rarely are these abusive police officers held accountable in a court of law.

Every time a police officer shoots someone, especially a young, Black male, we still face the possibility of falling into the same cycle we have seen over and over again—additional senseless killings, a mass community outpouring of love, and a resurgence of violence as well as community dialogue.

The sad truth is that the Black community has long since pointed out the presence of police brutality. I may even dare to say that this has been a common topic of conversation for almost a century. And I am going to double down and continue to repeat the plea for wide-sweeping reform. Another truth is that reform is not going to occur until the ugliness of police brutality hits America in the heart. Until now, to most of America, police brutality has been seen as "your problem." But the protests over the last few years have proven that we are now calling it what it has always been: "our problem."

As we reflect on our experiences, we recognize the importance of celebrating Northern Kentucky's unique identity. Despite the overshadowing presence of our northern neighbor, Cincinnati, and the occasional neglect from our own state of Kentucky, we carry forward a legacy of pride, perseverance, and progress. Our stories are woven into the broader fabric of the region,

contributing to its diversity and strength. Our stories are intertwined with the struggles and triumphs of a community that has always fought to be seen and heard. Despite the small Black population in Northern Kentucky, we have created spaces of support, culture, and empowerment. From family gatherings and church events to local initiatives and friendships, we have built a tapestry of connection that has enriched our lives and anchored our sense of belonging.

Growing up in Northern Kentucky has instilled in me a profound sense of belonging and pride, and I feel a sense of responsibility to continue to share our stories, to highlight the rich heritage of my home, and to ensure that Northern Kentucky is recognized for its contributions and cherished for its distinct character. As I move forward, I do so with the knowledge that our voices matter and our experiences shape the narrative of a region that deserves to be remembered and celebrated.

As I conclude this book, it is clear that growing up in Northern Kentucky as Black male has left an indelible mark on who I am. It has taught me the value of community, the importance of perseverance, and the power of my voice. Moving forward, I carry with me the responsibility to share my story, to uplift the next generation, and to ensure that my experience contributes to the broader narrative of this unique region. In doing so, I honor my past and pave the way for a future in which every individual is recognized and celebrated.

Notes

Chapter 1

1. Eric R. Jackson, "Why So Many African Americans Have Roots in the West End of Cincinnati," Voice of Black Cincinnati, June 6, 2024, www.thevoiceofblackcincinnati.com.

Chapter 2

2. Barbara Blum and Deborah Rieselman, "The Taft Influence," *UC Magazine*, July 1999. www.magazine.uc.edu.
3. Creative Exchange, "ArtsWave Cincinnati Is the Oldest and Largest United Arts Fund in the Country," July 31, 2016, www.springboardexchange.org.
4. Gianna Samms, "5 Groundbreaking 19th-Century African American Artists," History, January 3, 2024, www.history.com.
5. WCPO 9 News, "Artist Duncanson's Sweeping, Complex Life," February 25, 2016, www.wcpo.com.
6. WCPO 9 News, "Duncanson's Sweeping, Complex Life."
7. WCPO 9 News, "Duncanson's Sweeping, Complex Life."

Chapter 3

8. Ohio History Connection, "Cincinnati Union Terminal," May 14, 2024, www.ohiohistory.org.
9. Mia Bay, "Jim Crow Journeys: An Excerpt from Traveling Black," *Southern Spaces*, June 7, 2021, www.southernspaces.org.
10. Jim Crow Museum, "Pullman Porters," 2021, www.jimcrowmuseum.ferris.edu.

Chapter 4

11. Joel M. Beall, "Cincinnati Icon: George 'Boss' Cox," March 11, 2015, Cincinnati.com, www.cincinnati.com.
12. Oxford Bibliographies, "African Americans in Cincinnati," August 25, 2021. www.oxfordbibliographies.com.
13. Beall, "Cincinnati Icon."
14. Walnut Hills Historical Society, "Riots of 1841," February 1, 2018, www.cincinnatihistory.org.
15. Course Hero, "George 'Boss' Cox Was Both a Liberator and a Tyrant During His Lifetime," March 13, 2022, www.coursehero.com.
16. *Encyclopedia Virginia*, "John Mercer Langston (1829–1897)," August 26, 2024, www.encyclopediavirginia.org.
17. Eric R. Jackson, "African American Political Leaders in Cincinnati Throughout History," Voice of Black Cincinnati, June 26, 2024, www.thevoiceofblackcincinnati.com.
18. Union Baptist Church, "A Church on the Move for Christ Since 1831," June 7, 2024, www.union-baptist.net.
19. Jackson, "African American Political Leaders."
20. Jackson, "African American Political Leaders."
21. Jackson, "African American Political Leaders."

Chapter 5

22. Bryan Greene, "America's First Black Physician Sought to Heal a Nation's Persistent Illness," *Smithsonian*, February 26, 2021, www.smithsonianmag.com.
23. Sarah Pruit, "What Did Jesus Look Like?," History, March 18, 2024, www.history.com.
24. Kareem A. Simpson, "These Sites Hold Stories of African American History in Northern Kentucky," *NKY Thrives*, January 23, 2020, www.nkythrives.com.

Chapter 6

25. PBS, "People & Ideas: Lyman Beecher," October 11, 2010, www.pbs.org.
26. Civil War on the Western Boarder, "Harriet Beecher Stowe Meets Lincoln," January 2000, www.civilwaronthewesternborder.org.
27. Ohio History Connection, "Harriet Beecher Stowe House," YouTube, August 24, 2023, www.youtube.com.
28. Oberlin Heritage Center, "Oberlin Heritage Center Blog: A Visit to the Harriet Beecher Stowe House," September 8, 2017, www.oberlinheritagecenter.org.

29. Kareem Simpson, "Bradley, James," *Northern Kentucky Encyclopedia* (University Press of Kentucky, 2009), 248–51.
30. National Park Service, "Oviatt House and Harriet Beecher Stowe House #TakeoverTheNetwork," September 13, 2022, www.nps.gov.

Chapter 7

31. NPR, "Bob Dylan, Toni Morrison Among Those Honored with Medal of Freedom," May 29, 2012, www.npr.org.
32. History, "Millard Fillmore Sworn in as 13th U.S. President," July 8, 2024, www.history.com.
33. African Americans of the Kentucky Borderlands, "Gaines, Abner," December 20, 2022, www.omekas.bcplhistory.org.
34. Kentucky Commission on Human Rights, "Margaret Garner," 2024, www.kchr.ky.gov.
35. Kentucky Commission on Human Rights, "Margaret Garner."
36. Kentucky Historical Society, "Modern Medea," 2024, www.explorekyhistory.ky.gov.

About the Author

Kareem A. Simpson is an American author, playwright, and creative visionary whose work challenges societal norms while illuminating untold stories of resilience, identity, and belonging. His literary and theatrical creations have resonated across the United States, with a particular impact in the greater Cincinnati/Northern Kentucky region.

Simpson's works include *Bro'Kin RIVER* (2021), a poignant sixty-minute stage play based on the true story of Margaret Garner, an enslaved woman in Northern Kentucky who chooses the unthinkable to protect her child from the horrors of enslavement. Another hallmark of his career is *Chronicles of a Boy Misunderstood* (2013), a groundbreaking exploration of Black gay identity through fictional narratives that fearlessly confront themes of love, social status, racism, and the LGBTQ experience.

As the founder and chief imagination officer of SparkLight Creative Group, Simpson inspires artists and creative entrepreneurs to develop their craft and transform their visions into meaningful ventures. His work has been showcased in prestigious collections, such as the *Northern Kentucky Encyclopedia*, and at significant conferences, including Railvolution's National Conference and the Kentucky Association of Blacks in Higher Education. Locally, his storytelling enriches greater Cincinnati outlets, like *SoapBox Cincinnati*, *NKY Thrives*, and the *River City News*.

In 2023, Simpson was honored as the Kenton County Public Library's writer-in-residence. His accolades include being a finalist for the 2022 NKY PRIDE Community Award and receiving the Northern Kentucky NAACP's

2020 President's Award for advancing Black voices through personal and professional development. That same year, he earned the Heart of the Community Award for his dedication to improving Covington and uplifting its residents.

With a passion for challenging narratives and inspiring change, Simpson continues to create works that connect deeply with audiences, fostering dialogue around race, identity, and community.